# everyday Italian

# everyday Italian

MURDOCH
BOOKS

# contents

# antipasto

# MARINATED BOCCONCINI

Preparation time: 15 minutes +
 3 days refrigeration
Total cooking time: 5 minutes
Serves 8

400 g (13 oz) bocconcini, sliced
150 g (5 oz) sun-dried capsicums in oil
1 cup (50 g/1¾ oz) small fresh basil
 leaves
1¼ cups (315 ml/10 fl oz) extra virgin
 olive oil
¼ cup (60 ml/2 fl oz) lemon juice

**1** Dry the bocconcini with paper towels. Drain the capsicums, retaining the oil in a pan, and cut into strips. Gently crush the basil leaves. Pour 1 cup (250 ml/8 fl oz) of the olive oil into the pan with the capsicum oil and gently heat for 5 minutes. Stir the lemon juice into the warmed oil.
**2** Put a layer of bocconcini slices in a wide-necked 3-cup (750 ml/24 fl oz) sterilised clip-top jar. Sprinkle with cracked pepper. Put a thin layer of basil leaves on top of the cheese and cover with some of the capsicum. Continue layering, then cover with the warmed oil, using the remaining olive oil if necessary. Seal the jar and marinate in the refrigerator for 3 days. Return to room temperature and drain before serving.

NUTRITION PER SERVE
Protein 13 g; Fat 25 g; Carbohydrate 1 g;
Dietary Fibre 0 g; Cholesterol 30 mg;
1194 kJ (285 cal)

NOTE: To sterilise a storage jar, rinse with boiling water then place in a warm oven until completely dry. Don't dry with a tea towel.

Drain the oil from the sun-dried capsicums into a small pan.

Gently crush the basil leaves with a knife to release more of the flavour.

Layer the bocconcini, basil and capsicum and then cover with the warmed oil.

## SEMI-DRIED TOMATOES

Preparation time: 10 minutes +
    24 hours refrigeration
Total cooking time: 2 hours 30 minutes
Fills a 500 ml (16 fl oz) jar

16 Roma tomatoes
3 tablespoons fresh thyme, chopped
2 tablespoons olive oil

**1** Preheat the oven to warm 160°C (315°F/Gas 2–3). Cut the tomatoes into quarters lengthways and lay them skin-side-down on a wire rack in a baking tray.
**2** Sprinkle with 1 teaspoon of salt, 1 teaspoon of cracked black pepper and the thyme and cook in the oven for 2$1/2$ hours. Check occasionally to make sure the tomatoes don't burn.
**3** Toss the tomatoes in the olive oil and leave to cool before packing into sterilised jars and sealing. Store in the refrigerator for 24 hours before using. Semi-dried tomatoes should be eaten within 3–4 days.

NUTRITION
Analysis is not appropriate for this recipe.

NOTE: To sterilise a storage jar, rinse with boiling water, then place in a warm oven until completely dry. Do not dry with a tea towel.

Cut the tomatoes into quarters and lay them skin-side-down on a wire rack.

Season the tomatoes with salt, cracked pepper and fresh thyme.

Cover the tomatoes with olive oil and toss until well coated.

# SARDINES WITH CHARGRILLED CAPSICUM AND EGGPLANT

Preparation time: 25 minutes
Total cooking time: 35 minutes
Serves 4

2 large red capsicums, quartered
    and seeded
4 finger eggplants, cut into quarters
    lengthways
cooking oil spray
16 fresh sardines, butterflied
    (about 300 g/10 oz)
1 slice white bread, crusts removed
1/3 cup (7 g/1/4 oz) fresh parsley
1 clove garlic, crushed
1 teaspoon grated lemon rind

DRESSING
1 tablespoon olive oil
1 tablespoon balsamic vinegar
1/2 teaspoon soft brown sugar
1 clove garlic, crushed
1 tablespoon chopped fresh chives

**1** Preheat the oven to moderate 180°C (350°F/Gas 4). Lightly grease a large baking dish with oil. Preheat the grill and line with foil.
**2** Grill or barbecue the capsicum until the skin is blistered and blackened. Cool under a damp tea towel, peel and slice thickly lengthways. Lightly spray the eggplant with oil and grill or barbecue each side for 3–5 minutes, until softened.
**3** Combine the dressing ingredients in a jar and shake well. Put the capsicum and eggplant in a bowl, pour the dressing over and toss well.
**4** Place the sardines on a baking tray in a single layer, well spaced. Finely chop the bread, parsley, garlic and lemon rind together in a food processor. Sprinkle over each sardine. Bake for 10–15 minutes, until cooked through. Serve the capsicum and eggplant topped with sardines.

NUTRITION PER SERVE
Protein 20 g; Fat 15 g; Carbohydrate 15 g;
Dietary Fibre 3 g; Cholesterol 85 mg;
1185 kJ (285 Cal)

When the capsicum has cooled enough to handle, peel away the skin.

Pour the dressing over the capsicum and eggplant, then toss.

Sprinkle the chopped bread, parsley, garlic and lemon rind over the sardines.

# FENNEL WITH PECORINO CHEESE

Preparation time: 15 minutes
Total cooking time: 25 minutes
Serves 4

4 fennel bulbs
1 clove garlic, crushed
1/2 lemon, sliced
2 tablespoons olive oil
1 teaspoon salt

3 tablespoons butter, melted
2 tablespoons grated Pecorino
cheese

**1** Cut the top shoots and base off the fennel and remove the tough outer layers. Cut into segments and place in a pan with the garlic, lemon, oil and salt. Cover with water and bring to the boil. Reduce the heat and simmer for 20 minutes, or until just tender.
**2** Drain well and place in a heatproof dish. Drizzle with the butter. Sprinkle with the cheese and season to taste.
**3** Place under a preheated grill until the cheese has browned. Best served piping hot.

NUTRITION PER SERVE
Protein 4 g; Fat 23 g; Carbohydrate 3 g;
Dietary Fibre 2.5 g; Cholesterol 43 mg;
990 kJ (235 Cal)

NOTE: If Pecorino (a hard sheep's milk cheese) is not available, use Parmesan instead.

Trim the tops and bases from the fennel and remove the tough outer layers.

Cut the fennel into segments and put in a pan with the garlic, lemon, oil and salt.

Sprinkle grated Pecorino cheese over the fennel and brown under a grill.

# Bruschetta

To make basic bruschetta, cut a crusty Italian loaf into twelve 1.5 cm (5/8 inch) diagonal slices. Toast or grill the slices until golden. Bruise 2 garlic cloves with the flat of a knife, peel and rub the cloves over both sides of the hot bread. Drizzle the tops with a little extra virgin olive oil and finish with one of these delicious toppings.

### ANCHOVY, TOMATO AND OREGANO

Seed and roughly chop 3 vine-ripened tomatoes and mix with 1 small chopped red onion, a 90 g (3 oz) jar drained, minced anchovy fillets and 2 tablespoons olive oil. Spoon some of the mixture onto each bruschetta. Drizzle with extra virgin olive oil, and garnish with chopped fresh oregano and freshly ground black pepper.

### BLACK OLIVE PATE, ROCKET AND FETA

Place 100 g (3½ oz) trimmed baby rocket leaves, 75 g (2½ oz) crumbled Greek feta and 2 tablespoons olive oil in a bowl, and mix together well. Spread 2 teaspoons of black olive pâté onto each bruschetta slice and top with the feta mixture. Drizzle with extra virgin olive oil and season with sea salt and freshly ground black pepper.

### SUN-DRIED TOMATO PESTO, ARTICHOKE AND BOCCONCINI

Spread 1 teaspoon of good-quality sun-dried tomato pesto onto each slice of bruschetta. Slice 12 (360 g/ 12 oz) bocconcini and place on top of the pesto. Chop 55 g (2 oz) drained marinated artichoke hearts in oil and place over the bocconcini slices. Sprinkle with some finely chopped fresh flat-leaf parsley.

## PESTO, RED CAPSICUM AND PARMESAN

Cut 3 medium red capsicums into large flattish pieces and remove the seeds and membrane. Cook the capsicum pieces, skin-side-up, under a hot grill until the skin blackens and blisters. Place in a plastic bag and leave to cool. When cool enough to handle, peel away the skin. Discard the skin and cut the flesh into 1 cm (1/2 inch) strips. Spread 2 teaspoons good-quality basil pesto onto each slice of the bruschetta. Top with the red capsicum strips and 50 g (1 3/4 oz) fresh Parmesan shards. Drizzle with extra virgin olive oil and season with sea salt and ground black pepper.

## MUSHROOM AND GOAT'S CHEESE

Preheat the oven to moderate 180°C (350°F/Gas 4). Mix 1/2 cup (125 ml/ 4 fl oz) olive oil with 3 chopped garlic cloves, 2 tablespoons chopped fresh flat-leaf parsley and 1 tablespoon dry sherry. Place 6 large field mushrooms on a foil-lined baking tray and spoon on all but 2 tablespoons of the mixture. Bake for 20 minutes, or until soft. Mix 150 g (5 oz) goat's cheese with 1 teaspoon chopped fresh thyme, then spread over the bruschetta. Warm the remaining oil mixture. Cut the mushrooms in half and place one half on each bruschetta. Drizzle with the remaining oil. Season with sea salt and ground black pepper.

## TOMATO AND BASIL

Place 4 seeded and roughly chopped large vine-ripened tomatoes, 1/2 cup (15 g/1/2 oz) roughly torn fresh basil leaves, 2 tablespoons olive oil and 1/2 teaspoon caster sugar in a bowl and mix together well. Season with plenty of sea salt and black pepper and set the mixture aside for 10–15 minutes so the flavours have time to infuse and develop. Cut a ripe vine-ripened tomato in half and rub it on the oiled side of the slices of bruschetta, squeezing the tomato to extract as much of the liquid as possible. Carefully spoon 2 tablespoons of the tomato mixture onto each slice of bruschetta and serve immediately.

Left to right: Anchovy, tomato and oregano bruschetta; Black olive pâté, rocket and feta bruschetta; Sun-dried tomato pesto, artichoke and bocconcini bruschetta; Pesto, red capsicum and Parmesan bruschetta; Mushroom and goat's cheese bruschetta; Tomato and basil bruschetta.

## ROASTED BALSAMIC ONIONS

Preparation time: 15 minutes +
  overnight refrigeration
Total cooking time: 1 hour 30 minutes
Serves 8

1 kg (2 lb) pickling onions, unpeeled
  (see NOTE)
3/4 cup (185 ml/6 fl oz) balsamic
  vinegar
2 tablespoons soft brown sugar
3/4 cup (185 ml/6 fl oz) olive oil

**1** Preheat the oven to warm 160°C (315°F/Gas 2–3). Place the unpeeled onions in a baking dish and roast for 1½ hours. Leave until cool enough to handle. Trim the stems from the onions and peel away the skin (the outer part of the root should come away but the onions will remain intact). Rinse a 1-litre wide-necked jar with boiling water and dry in a warm oven (do not dry with a tea towel). Put the onions in the jar.
**2** Combine the vinegar and sugar in a small screw-top jar and stir to dissolve the sugar. Add the oil, seal the jar and shake vigorously until combined—the mixture will be paler and may separate on standing.
**3** Pour the vinegar mixture over the onions, seal, and turn upside down to coat. Marinate overnight in the refrigerator, turning occasionally. Return to room temperature and shake before serving.

NUTRITION PER SERVE
Protein 0.5 g; Fat 7.5 g; Carbohydrate 20 g;
Dietary Fibre 2 g; Cholesterol 0 mg;
677 kJ (162 cal)

NOTE: Pickling onions are very small, usually packed in 1 kg (2 lb) bags. The ideal size is around 35 g (1¼ oz) each. The sizes in the bag will probably range from 20 g (3/4 oz) up to 40 g (1¼ oz). The cooking time given is suitable for this range and there is no need to cook the larger ones for any longer. The marinating time given is a minimum time and the onions may be marinated for up to 3 days in the refrigerator. The marinade may separate after a few hours, which is fine—simply stir occasionally.

When cool, trim the stems from the onions and peel away the skin.

Add the oil to the vinegar and sugar and shake vigorously to combine.

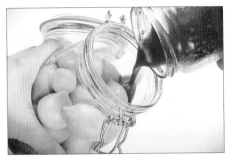

Pour the vinegar mixture over the onions, turning the jar to coat thoroughly.

# MARINATED CHILLI MUSHROOMS

Preparation time: 20 minutes +
  overnight refrigeration
Total cooking time: Nil
Serves 8 (as part of an antipasto
  platter, see HINT)

750 g (1¹/₂ lb) button mushrooms
2 cups (500 ml/16 fl oz) light olive oil
2 tablespoons lemon juice
1 clove garlic, finely chopped
¹/₄ teaspoon caster sugar

1 red chilli, finely chopped
1 green chilli, finely chopped
1 tablespoon chopped fresh coriander
1 tablespoon chopped fresh flat-leaf
  parsley

**1** Wipe the mushrooms clean with a damp paper towel and put in a bowl.
**2** Mix together the oil, lemon juice, garlic, sugar and chilli. Pour over the mushrooms and mix well. Cover with plastic wrap and marinate in the refrigerator overnight.
**3** Just before serving, add the herbs, season and mix well.

NUTRITION PER SERVE
Protein 3.5 g; Fat 1.5 g; Carbohydrate 2 g;
Dietary Fibre 2.5 g; Cholesterol 0 mg;
150 kJ (35 cal)

NOTE: The coriander and parsley are added just before serving so that they keep their colour. If you prefer a stronger flavour, add them before marinating.

HINT: Serve as part of an antipasto platter, with a selection of sun-dried vegetables, marinated artichokes, caperberries and toasted bruschetta.

Wipe the mushrooms with a damp paper towel to remove any dirt.

Pour the combined oil, lemon juice, garlic, sugar and chilli over the mushrooms.

Chop the coriander and parsley and add to the mushrooms just before serving.

# TOMATO AND BOCCONCINI SALAD

Preparation time: 10 minutes
Total cooking time: Nil
Serves 4

3 large vine-ripened tomatoes
250 g (8 oz) bocconcini
    (see NOTE)
12 fresh basil leaves
¼ cup (60 ml/2 fl oz) extra virgin
    olive oil
4 basil leaves, roughly torn, extra,

**1** Slice the tomatoes into 1 cm (½ inch) slices, making twelve slices altogether. Slice the bocconcini into twenty-four 1 cm (½ inch) slices.
**2** Arrange the tomato slices on a serving plate, alternating them with 2 slices of bocconcini. Place the basil leaves between the bocconcini slices.
**3** Drizzle with the oil, sprinkle with the basil and season well with salt and freshly ground black pepper.

NUTRITION PER SERVE
Protein 14 g; Fat 25 g; Carbohydrate 3 g; Dietary Fibre 1 g; Cholesterol 33 mg; 1221 kJ (292 Cal)

NOTE: This popular summer salad is most successful with very fresh buffalo mozzarella if you can find it. We've used bocconcini in this recipe as it can be difficult to find very fresh mozzarella.

Slice the bocconcini into twenty-four 1 cm (½ inch) thick slices.

Arrange the tomato slices on a serving plate, alternating with the bocconcini.

# INVOLTINI OF SWORDFISH

Preparation time: 30 minutes
Total cooking time: 10 minutes
Serves 4

1 kg (2 lb) swordfish, skin removed,
    cut into four 5 cm (2 inch) pieces
3 lemons
4 tablespoons olive oil
1 small onion, chopped
3 cloves garlic, chopped
2 tablespoons chopped capers
2 tablespoons chopped pitted
    Kalamata olives
1/3 cup (35 g/1 oz) finely grated
    Parmesan
1 1/2 cups (120 g/4 oz) fresh
    breadcrumbs
2 tablespoons chopped fresh parsley
1 egg, lightly beaten
24 fresh bay leaves
2 small white onions, quartered and
    separated into pieces
2 tablespoons lemon juice, extra

**1** Cut each swordfish piece horizontally into four slices to give you 16 slices. Place each piece between two pieces of plastic wrap and roll gently with a rolling pin to flatten without tearing. Cut each piece in half to give 32 pieces.
**2** Peel the lemons with a vegetable peeler. Cut the peel into 24 even pieces. Squeeze the lemons to give 3 tablespoons of juice.
**3** Heat 2 tablespoons olive oil in a pan, add the onion and garlic, and cook over medium heat for 2 minutes. Place in a bowl with the capers, olives, Parmesan, breadcrumbs and parsley. Season, add the egg and mix to bind.
**4** Divide the stuffing among the fish

pieces and, with oiled hands, roll up to form parcels. Thread four rolls onto each of eight skewers alternating with the bay leaves, lemon peel and onion.
**5** Mix the remaining oil with the lemon juice in a small bowl. Cook the skewers on a hot barbecue flatplate for 3–4 minutes each side, basting with

the oil and lemon mixture. Serve with a little extra lemon juice drizzled over the top.

NUTRITION PER SERVE
Protein 34 g; Fat 38 g; Carbohydrate 5.5 g;
Dietary Fibre 5 g; Cholesterol 193 mg;
2065 kJ (493 cal)

Roll the swordfish out between two pieces of plastic wrap.

Roll up the fish pieces and filling with oiled hands to form neat parcels.

Thread the rolls, bay leaves, lemon peel and onion onto skewers.

## CAPONATA

Preparation time: 20 minutes +
  24 hours refrigeration
Total cooking time: 40 minutes
Serves 8

1 kg (2 lb) eggplant, cubed
3/4 cup (185 ml/6 fl oz) olive oil
200 g (6½ oz) zucchini, cubed
1 red capsicum, thinly sliced
2 onions, finely sliced
4 celery sticks, sliced
400 g (13 oz) can crushed tomatoes
3 tablespoons red wine vinegar
2 tablespoons sugar
2 tablespoons drained capers
24 green olives, pitted (see NOTE)
2 tablespoons pine nuts, toasted

**1** Put the eggplant in a colander, sprinkle with salt and leave to drain.
**2** Heat 3 tablespoons of the oil in a large frying pan and fry the zucchini and capsicum for 5–6 minutes, or until the zucchini is lightly browned. Transfer to a bowl. Add a little more oil to the pan and gently fry the onion and celery for 6–8 minutes, or until softened but not brown. Transfer to the bowl.
**3** Rinse the eggplant and pat dry. Add ¼ cup (60 ml/2 fl oz) of the oil to the pan, increase the heat and brown the eggplant in batches. Keep adding more oil to each batch. Drain on paper towels and set aside.
**4** Remove any excess oil from the pan and return the vegetables to the pan, except the eggplant.
**5** Add ¼ cup (60 ml/2 fl oz) water and the tomatoes. Reduce the heat and simmer for 10 minutes. Add the remaining ingredients and eggplant and mix well. Remove from the

heat and cool. Cover and leave for 24 hours in the refrigerator. Add some pepper, and more vinegar if needed.

NUTRITION PER SERVE
Protein 3.5 g; Fat 25 g; Carbohydrate 8.5 g; Dietary Fibre 5.5 g; Cholesterol 0 mg; 1160 kJ (280 cal)

NOTE: Green olives stuffed with red pimentos can be used instead of pitted green olives.

STORAGE TIME: Caponata will keep, covered, in the refrigerator for up to 5 days.

You can remove the stones from the olives with an olive pitter.

Increase the heat under the oil and brown the eggplant in batches.

Add the water and crushed tomatoes to the pan and allow to simmer.

# GARLIC AND HERB MARINATED ARTICHOKES

Preparation time: 20 minutes +
  overnight refrigeration
Total cooking time: Nil
Serves 8 (as part of an antipasto
  platter)

2 cloves garlic, chopped
1/2 cup (125 ml/4 fl oz) olive oil
2 tablespoons finely chopped
  fresh dill

3 tablespoons finely chopped fresh
  parsley
2 tablespoons finely chopped fresh
  basil
2 tablespoons lemon juice
2 x 400 g (13 oz) canned artichokes
1/4 cup (40 g/1 1/4 oz) finely diced
  red capsicum

**1** To make the marinade, whisk
together the garlic, oil, herbs and
lemon juice in a bowl. Season with salt
and cracked black pepper.
**2** Drain the artichokes and add to
the bowl with the capsicum. Mix well
to coat. Cover and marinate in the
refrigerator overnight. Serve as part of
an antipasto platter or use in salads.

NUTRITION PER SERVE
Protein 1 g; Fat 7.5 g; Carbohydrate 1 g;
Dietary Fibre 1.5 g; Cholesterol 0 mg;
320 kJ (75 cal)

STORAGE TIME: The artichokes will
keep in an airtight container in the
refrigerator for up to 1 week.

Finely chop the fresh herbs. You will need dill,
parsley and basil.

Combine the garlic, oil, herbs and lemon juice to
make the marinade.

Drain the artichokes well before adding to the
marinade. Marinate in the fridge overnight.

# SUMMER BREAD SALAD

Preparation time: 20 minutes
Total cooking time: 15 minutes
Serves 6–8

2 red capsicums
2 yellow capsicums
6 Roma (egg) tomatoes,
    cut into large chunks
100 g (3½ oz) capers, drained
100 g (3½ oz) black olives
150 g (5 oz) bocconcini, halved
1 Italian wood-fired loaf
2 cups (60 g/2 oz) basil leaves

DRESSING
4 cloves garlic, finely chopped
¼ cup (60 ml/2 fl oz) red wine vinegar
½ cup (125 ml/4 fl oz) extra virgin
    olive oil

**1** Cut the capsicums into large pieces, removing the seeds and membrane. Place, skin-side-up, under a hot grill, until the skin blackens and blisters. Cool in a plastic bag or under a tea towel, then peel away the skin and cut into thick strips.
**2** Put the capsicum, tomato, capers, olives and bocconcini in a bowl and toss to combine.

**3** Put the dressing ingredients in a screw-top jar and shake well.
**4** Cut the bread into large pieces and put in a bowl. Drizzle with the dressing and mix until well coated. Toss gently with the capsicum mixture and basil leaves.

NUTRITION PER SERVE (8)
Protein 15 g; Fat 25 g; Carbohydrate 35 g;
Dietary Fibre 4 g; Cholesterol 25 mg;
1870 kJ (445 Cal)

NOTE: This dish is based on the Tuscan favourite that uses leftover crusty bread to make a salad.

Put the grilled capsicum pieces in a plastic bag until cool enough to handle.

Put the grilled capsicum, tomato, capers, olives and bocconcini in a bowl and toss together.

Using a bread knife, cut the wood-fired loaf into large pieces.

# CHARGRILLED VEGETABLE TERRINE

Preparation time: 30 minutes +
  overnight refrigeration
Total cooking time: Nil
Serves 8

350 g (11 oz) ricotta cheese
2 cloves garlic, crushed
8 large slices chargrilled eggplant,
  drained (see NOTE)
10 slices chargrilled red capsicum,
  drained (see NOTE)
8 slices chargrilled zucchini, drained
  (see NOTE)
45 g (1½ oz) rocket leaves
3 marinated artichokes, drained and
  sliced
85 g (3 oz) semi-dried tomatoes,
  drained and chopped
100 g (3½ oz) marinated mushrooms,
  drained and halved

**1** Beat together the ricotta and garlic until smooth. Season well and set aside. Line a 23½ x 13 x 6½ cm (9 x 5 x 2½ inch) loaf tin with plastic wrap, leaving a generous amount hanging over the sides.
**2** Line the base of the tin with half the eggplant, cutting and fitting to cover the base. Top with a layer of half the capsicum, then all the zucchini slices. Spread evenly with the ricotta mixture and press down firmly. Place the rocket leaves on top of the ricotta. Arrange the artichoke, tomato and mushrooms in three rows lengthways on top of the ricotta.
**3** Top with another layer of capsicum and finish with the eggplant. Cover securely with the overhanging plastic wrap. Put a piece of cardboard on top and weigh it down with weights or small food cans. Refrigerate overnight.
**4** To serve, peel back the plastic wrap and turn the terrine out onto a plate. Remove the plastic wrap and cut into thick slices to serve.

NUTRITION PER SERVE
Protein 6 g; Fat 5 g; Carbohydrate 3 g; Dietary Fibre 2 g; Cholesterol 20 mg; 350 kJ (85 cal)

NOTE: You will find chargrilled vegetables at your local delicatessen. Alternatively, make your own by slicing the vegetables, brushing with oil and cooking on a barbecue or chargrill pan until lightly browned. Remove the skin from the capsicum first, by blackening it under a hot grill, then leaving in a plastic bag until the skin will peel away easily.

Put the ricotta and crushed garlic in a bowl and beat until smooth.

Arrange the mushrooms, tomato and artichoke in three rows over the rocket.

Cover the terrine with cardboard and weigh down with small food cans.

# Marinated Olives

Marinated olives are delicious on their own or as part of an antipasto platter, and will generally keep in the fridge for up to 6 months. To successfully store the olives, it is important to sterilise the storage jar first by rinsing it with boiling water and putting it in a warm oven to dry (don't use a tea towel).

### CITRUS HERBED OLIVES

Combine the julienned zest and juice of 1 orange and 1 lemon in a wide-necked, 750 ml (24 fl oz) sterilised jar. Add 1 tablespoon fresh thyme leaves, 2 tablespoons fresh oregano leaves, 1 crushed clove garlic and 1 tablespoon extra virgin olive oil. Seal and shake. Add 2 cups (370 g/ 12 oz) rinsed Kalamata olives and turn the jar to coat the olives, then add more oil to fully cover the olives. Marinate for 1–2 weeks in the refrigerator. Store in the refrigerator but bring back to room temperature before serving.

### LEMON AND CHILLI GREEN OLIVES

Place 2 teaspoons chopped red chilli, the julienned zest and juice of 1 lemon, 2 teaspoons sugar, 1 crushed clove garlic and 2 tablespoons extra virgin olive oil in a wide-necked, 750 ml (24 fl oz) sterilised jar. Seal and shake well to combine the ingredients. Add 2 cups (450 g/14 oz) rinsed large green olives and turn the jar to coat the olives, adding more oil to fully cover. Seal and marinate in the refrigerator for 1–2 weeks. Store in the refrigerator but serve at room temperature.

### DILL AND LEMON OLIVES

Finely slice half a lemon and cut the slices into wedges. Rinse and drain 500 g (1 lb) Riviera or Ligurian olives. Layer the olives in a wide-necked, 750 ml (24 fl oz) sterilised jar with 3–4 sprigs fresh dill, 1 teaspoon fennel seeds, 3 finely sliced cloves garlic and the lemon wedges. Pour in the juice of half a lemon and 1¾ cups (440 ml/ 14 fl oz) oil, or enough to cover the olives. Seal and marinate in the refrigerator for 1–2 weeks before using. Store in the refrigerator. Return to room temperature before serving.

## SUN-DRIED TOMATO OLIVES

Rinse and drain 500 g (1 lb) black olives. Cut two slits into each olive. Layer in a wide-necked, 750 ml (24 fl oz) sterilised jar with 100 g (3½ oz) drained and chopped sun-dried tomatoes in oil (reserve the oil), 2 crushed cloves garlic, 2 bay leaves and 3 teaspoons fresh thyme leaves. Add 1 tablespoon red wine vinegar and 1 cup (250 ml/8 fl oz) oil (use the reserved sun-dried tomato oil) or enough to cover the olives. Shake well, seal and leave to marinate in the refrigerator for 1–2 weeks. Store in the refrigerator and return to room temperature before serving.

## OLIVES WITH HERBS DE PROVENCE

Rinse and drain 500 g (1 lb) Niçoise or Ligurian olives. Put 1 crushed clove garlic, 2 teaspoons chopped fresh basil, 1 teaspoon each chopped fresh thyme, rosemary, marjoram, oregano and mint, 1 teaspoon fennel seeds, 2 tablespoons lemon juice and ½ cup (125 ml/4 fl oz) olive oil in a bowl and mix together. Put the olives and marinade in a wide-necked, 750 ml (24 fl oz) sterilised jar, adding extra olive oil to cover the olives. Seal and shake. Marinate in the refrigerator for 1–2 weeks. Store in the refrigerator but serve at room temperature.

## HONEY CITRUS OLIVES

Mix together the zest of 1 lemon, lime and orange, 2 tablespoons lime juice, 4 tablespoons lemon juice, 1 tablespoon orange juice, 1 tablespoon honey, 2 teaspoons wholegrain mustard, ½ cup (125 ml/4 fl oz) extra virgin olive oil, 2 thinly sliced cloves garlic, ¼ teaspoon dried oregano or 1 tablespoon chopped fresh oregano leaves and 6 thin slices of lemon and lime. Add 1½ cups (265 g/8½ oz) drained unpitted black olives, 1½ cups (265 g/8½ oz) drained unpitted green olives, 2 tablespoons chopped fresh parsley, salt and pepper. Place in a wide-necked, 750 ml (24 fl oz) sterilised jar and seal. Shake, then marinate in the refrigerator for 1–2 weeks. Store in the refrigerator but serve at room temperature.

## LEMON OLIVES WITH VERMOUTH

Rinse and drain 340 g (11 oz) whole green or stuffed olives. Layer in a wide-necked, 750 ml (24 fl oz) sterilised jar with ½ cup (125 ml/4 fl oz) dry vermouth, 2 tablespoons lemon juice, 1 tablespoon shredded lemon rind and ⅓ cup (80 ml/2¾ fl oz) extra virgin olive oil. Shake well, seal and marinate in the refrigerator overnight. Store in the refrigerator but return to room temperature before serving.

From left to right: Citrus herbed olives; Lemon and chilli green olives; Sun-dried tomato olives; Dill and lemon olives; Olives with herbs de Provence; Honey citrus olives; Lemon olives with vermouth.

# soups & stews

# MINESTRONE WITH PESTO

Preparation time: 25 minutes
  + overnight soaking
Total cooking time: 2 hours
Serves 6

125 g (4 oz) dried borlotti beans
1 large onion, roughly chopped
2 cloves garlic
3 tablespoons chopped fresh parsley
60 g (2 oz) pancetta, chopped
3 tablespoons olive oil
1 celery stick, halved lengthways, then
  cut into 1 cm (1/2 inch) slices
1 carrot, halved lengthways, then cut
  into 1 cm (1/2 inch) slices
1 potato, diced
2 teaspoons tomato paste
400 g (12 oz) can crushed tomatoes
6 fresh basil leaves, roughly torn
2 litres chicken or vegetable stock
2 thin zucchini, cut into thick slices
3/4 cup (120 g/4 oz) shelled fresh peas
60 g (2 oz) green beans, cut into
  short lengths
90 g (3 oz) silverbeet leaves, shredded
75 g (21/2 oz) ditalini or other small
  pasta

PESTO
1 cup (30 g/1 oz) loosely packed fresh
  basil leaves
1 tablespoon lightly toasted pine nuts
2 cloves garlic
100 ml (31/2 fl oz) olive oil
1/4 cup (30 g/2 oz) grated Parmesan

**1**  Put the beans in a large bowl, cover with water and soak overnight. Drain and rinse under cold water.
**2**  Put the onion, garlic, parsley and pancetta in a food processor and process until fine. Heat the oil in a saucepan, add the pancetta mixture and cook over low heat, stirring occasionally, for 8–10 minutes.
**3**  Add the celery, carrot and potato, and cook for 5 minutes, then stir in the tomato paste, tomato, basil and borlotti beans. Season with freshly ground black pepper. Add the stock and bring slowly to the boil. Cover and simmer, stirring occasionally, for 1 hour 30 minutes.
**4**  Season and add the zucchini, peas, green beans, silverbeet and pasta. Simmer for 8–10 minutes, or until the vegetables and pasta are *al dente*.
**5**  To make the pesto, combine the basil, pine nuts and garlic with a pinch of salt in a food processor. Process until finely chopped. With the motor running, slowly add the olive oil. Transfer to a bowl and stir in the Parmesan and freshly ground black pepper to taste. Serve the soup in bowls with the pesto on top.

NUTRITION PER SERVE
Protein 9 g; Fat 30 g; Carbohydrate 20 g;
Dietary Fibre 5.3 g; Cholesterol 9 mg;
1593 kJ (380 cal)

Cook the processed onion, garlic, parsley and pancetta mixture.

Simmer until the pasta and vegetables are *al dente*.

Stir the Parmesan and black pepper into the pesto and serve with the soup.

## OSSO BUCO WITH GREMOLATA

Preparation time: 30 minutes
Total cooking time: 2 hours 40 minutes
Serves 4

2 tablespoons olive oil
1 onion, finely chopped
1 clove garlic, crushed
1 kg (2 lb) veal shin slices
   (osso buco)
2 tablespoons plain flour
410 g (13 oz) can tomatoes, roughly
   chopped
1 cup (250 ml/8 fl oz) white wine
1 cup (250 ml/8 fl oz) chicken
   stock

GREMOLATA
2 tablespoons finely choppped fresh
   parsley
2 teaspoons grated lemon rind
1 teaspoon finely chopped garlic

**1** Heat 1 tablespoon oil in a large shallow casserole. Add the onion and cook over low heat until soft and golden. Add the garlic. Cook for 1 minute, then remove from the dish.
**2** Heat the remaining oil and brown the veal in batches, then remove. Return the onion to the casserole and stir in the flour. Cook for 30 seconds and remove from the heat. Slowly stir in the tomatoes, wine and stock, combining well with the flour. Return the veal to the casserole.

**3** Return to the heat and bring to the boil, stirring. Cover and reduce the heat to low so that the casserole is just simmering. Cook for 2½ hours, or until the meat is very tender and almost falling off the bones.
**4** To make the gremolata, combine the parsley, lemon rind and garlic in a bowl. Sprinkle over the osso buco and serve with risotto or plain rice.

NUTRITION PER SERVE
Protein 50 g; Fat 15 g; Carbohydrate 9.5 g;
Dietary Fibre 2.5 g; Cholesterol 165 mg;
1700 kJ (405 Cal)

HINT: Try to make this a day in advance to give the flavours time to develop and blend.

Heat the oil in the casserole and cook the veal pieces in batches until browned.

Add the tomatoes, white wine and stock and mix until well combined.

Make the traditional gremolata topping by mixing together the parsley, lemon rind and garlic.

## CHICKEN STEW WITH WHITE BEANS AND ZUCCHINI

Preparation time: 15 minutes
Total cooking time: 1 hour
Serves 4
Fat per serve: 8 g

1 tablespoon olive oil
8 chicken thigh cutlets
1 onion, halved, thinly sliced
4 cloves garlic, finely chopped
3 tablespoons white wine
1 cup (250 ml/8 fl oz) chicken stock
1 tablespoon finely chopped fresh
   rosemary

1 teaspoon grated lemon rind
1 bay leaf
2 x 400 g (13 oz) cans cannellini
   beans, rinsed and drained
3 zucchini, halved lengthways, cut on
   the diagonal

**1** Heat the oil in a large flameproof casserole dish. Add the chicken, in batches, and cook for 4 minutes each side or until browned. Remove.
**2** Add the onion to the dish and cook for 5 minutes, or until soft. Add the garlic and cook for 1 minute, or until fragrant, then add the wine and chicken stock and bring to the boil, scraping the bottom of the pan to remove any sediment.

**3** Return the chicken and any juices to the pan along with the rosemary, lemon rind and bay leaf. Reduce the heat and simmer, covered, for 40 minutes, or until the chicken is tender. Stir in the cannellini beans and zucchini and cook for 5 minutes more, or until the zucchini is tender.

NUTRITION PER SERVE
Protein 37 g; Fat 8 g; Carbohydrate 25 g;
Dietary Fibre 15 g; Cholesterol 50 mg;
1394 kJ (334 cal)

STORAGE TIME: Can be frozen in snap-lock bags or an airtight container for up to 3 months.

Stir in the rinsed and drained cannellini beans and the zucchini and cook for 5 minutes more.

If you want to freeze this dish, transfer to snap-lock bags or an airtight container.

Brown the chicken thigh cutlets in batches in a large casserole dish.

# MEDITERRANEAN LAMB CASSEROLE

Preparation time: 15 minutes
Total cooking time: 1 hour
Serves 4

1 tablespoon olive oil
750 g (1¹/₂ lb) lamb from the bone,
   diced
1 large onion, sliced
2 cloves garlic, crushed
2 carrots, chopped
2 parsnips, chopped
400 g (13 oz) can chopped tomatoes
2 tablespoons tomato paste
2 teaspoons chopped fresh rosemary
¹/₂ cup (125 ml/4 fl oz) red wine
1 cup (250 ml/8 fl oz) chicken stock

**1** Heat the oil in a large saucepan and cook the lamb, in batches, for 3–4 minutes, or until browned. Remove from the pan and keep warm. Add the onion and garlic to the pan and cook for 2–3 minutes, or until the onion is soft.
**2** Return the lamb and juices to the pan. Add the carrots, parsnips, tomatoes, tomato paste, rosemary, wine and stock and bring to the boil. Reduce the heat and cover the pan. Simmer the casserole for 50 minutes, or until the lamb is tender and the sauce has thickened. Serve with soft polenta or couscous.

NUTRITION PER SERVE
Protein 45 g; Fat 12 g; Carbohydrate 12 g;
Dietary Fibre 4.5 g; Cholesterol 125 mg;
1517 kJ (362 Cal)

Add the onion and garlic to the pan and cook until the onion is soft.

Simmer until the lamb is tender and the sauce has thickened.

## BEAN SOUP WITH SAUSAGE

Preparation time: 25 minutes
Total cooking time: 25 minutes
Serves 4–6

2 teaspoons olive oil
4 Italian sausages, diced
2 leeks, sliced
1 clove garlic, crushed
1 large carrot, chopped into small cubes
2 celery stalks, sliced
2 tablespoons plain flour
2 beef stock cubes, crumbled
1/2 cup (125 ml/4 fl oz) white wine
125 g (4 oz) small pasta shells
440 g (14 oz) can three-bean mix, drained
1 teaspoon chopped chilli (optional)

**1** Heat the oil in a large heavy-based pan and add the sausage. Cook over medium heat for 5 minutes or until golden, stirring regularly. Drain on paper towels.
**2** Add the leek, garlic, carrot and celery to the pan and cook, stirring occasionally, for 2–3 minutes or until soft.
**3** Add the flour and cook, stirring, for 1 minute. Add the stock cube and wine and gradually stir in 2 litres of water. Bring to the boil, then reduce the heat and simmer for 10 minutes.
**4** Add the pasta, beans and chilli to the pan. Increase the heat and cook for 8–10 minutes, or until the pasta is *al dente*. Return the sausage to the soup and season to taste.

NUTRITION PER SERVE (6)
Protein 10 g; Fat 4 g; Carbohydrate 30 g; Dietary Fibre 8 g; Cholesterol 7 mg; 888 kJ (212 cal)

Cook the sausage pieces over medium heat for 5 minutes, or until golden.

Add the leek, garlic, carrot and celery and cook until soft.

Add the stock cubes and then the water and wine and bring to the boil.

Add the pasta, beans and chilli to the soup and cook until the pasta is tender.

## VEAL, LEMON AND CAPER STEW

Preparation time: 30 minutes
Total cooking time: 2 hours
Serves 6
Fat per serve: 13 g

1 tablespoon olive oil
50 g (1³/₄ oz) butter
1 kg (2 lb) stewing veal,
    cut into 4 cm (1¹/₂ inch) chunks
300 g (10 oz) French shallots
3 leeks, cut into large chunks
2 cloves garlic, crushed
1 tablespoon plain flour
2 cups (500 ml/16 fl oz)
    chicken stock
1 teaspoon grated lemon rind
¹/₃ cup (80 ml/2³/₄ fl oz) lemon juice
2 bay leaves
2 tablespoons capers, drained and
    well rinsed

**1** Heat the oil and half the butter in a large, heavy-based pan. Brown the veal in batches over medium-high heat and transfer to a large casserole dish.
**2** Blanch the shallots in boiling water for 30 seconds, then peel and add to the pan with the leeks. Gently cook for 5 minutes, or until soft and golden. Add the garlic, cook for 1 minute, then transfer to the casserole dish.
**3** Melt the remaining butter in the pan, add the flour and cook for 30 seconds. Remove from the heat, add the stock and stir until well combined. Return to the heat and cook, stirring, until the sauce begins to bubble.
**4** Pour the sauce into the casserole dish and stir in the lemon rind, lemon juice and bay leaves. Cover and cook over medium–low heat for 1–1¹/₂ hours, or until the veal is tender. During the last 20 minutes of cooking, remove the lid to allow the sauces to reduce a little. Stir in the capers and season with salt and pepper before serving.

NUTRITION PER SERVE
Protein 40 g; Fat 13 g; Carbohydrate 5 g;
Dietary Fibre 2 g; Cholesterol 160 mg;
1300 kJ (300 cal)

Add the leeks and peeled shallots to the pan and gently fry until soft and golden.

Remove the pan from the heat and stir in the stock, scraping up the brown bits.

## BACON AND PEA SOUP

Preparation time: 20 minutes
Total cooking time: 15 minutes
Serves 4–6

4 rashers bacon, diced
50 g (1¹/₂ oz) butter
1 large onion, finely chopped
1 celery stalk, chopped into small
     pieces
2 litres chicken stock

1 cup (150 g/5 oz) frozen peas
250 g (8 oz) risoni
2 tablespoons chopped fresh parsley

**1** Put the bacon, butter, onion and celery in a large heavy-based pan. Cook for 5 minutes over low heat, stirring occasionally.
**2** Add the stock and peas and simmer, covered, for 5 minutes. Increase the heat and add the pasta. Cook uncovered, stirring occasionally, for 5 minutes. Add the parsley and serve.

NUTRITION PER SERVE (6)
Protein 10 g; Fat 9 g; Carbohydrate 35 g;
Dietary Fibre 4 g; Cholesterol 28 mg;
1066 kJ (255 cal)

STORAGE: Store in an airtight container in the refrigerator for up to a day. Gently reheat before serving.
HINT: Double-smoked bacon will give the best flavour.

Remove the rind and any excess fat from the bacon before you dice it.

Cook the bacon, butter, onion and celery in a large pan for 5 minutes.

Just before you serve the soup, add the chopped parsley.

## SLOW-COOKED SHANKS

Preparation time: 20 minutes
Total cooking time: 3 hours
Serves 4

1 tablespoon oil
4 lamb shanks
2 red onions, sliced
10 cloves garlic, peeled
400 g (13 oz) can chopped tomatoes
1/2 cup (125 ml/4 fl oz) dry white wine
1 bay leaf

1 teaspoon grated lemon rind
1 large red capsicum, chopped
3 tablespoons chopped fresh parsley

**1** Heat the oil in a large flameproof casserole dish, add the shanks in batches and cook over high heat until browned on all sides. Return all the lamb to the casserole.
**2** Add the onion and garlic to the casserole and cook until softened. Add the tomato, wine, bay leaf, lemon rind, capsicum and 1/2 cup (125 ml/4 fl oz) water and bring to the boil.

**3** Cover the casserole and cook over medium–low heat for 2–2 1/2 hours, or until the meat is tender and falling off the bone and the sauce has thickened. Season to taste. Sprinkle the parsley over the top before serving. Serve with couscous or soft polenta.

NUTRITION PER SERVE
Protein 35 g; Fat 10 g; Carbohydrate 9 g;
Dietary Fibre 4.5 g; Cholesterol 85 mg;
1275 kJ (305 Cal)

Heat the oil in a pan and brown the lamb shanks in batches.

Add the onion and garlic to the casserole and cook until softened.

Add the tomato, wine, bay leaf, lemon rind, capsicum and water.

## MINESTRONE PRIMAVERA

Preparation time: 15 minutes
Total cooking time: 40 minutes
Serves 4–6

1/4 cup (60 ml/2 fl oz) olive oil
45 g (1 1/2 oz) pancetta, finely chopped
2 onions, chopped
2 cloves garlic, thinly sliced
2 small celery stalks, sliced
2 litres chicken stock
1/3 cup (50 g/1 3/4 oz) macaroni
2 zucchini, chopped
2 cups (150 g/5 oz) shredded savoy cabbage
1 1/2 cups (185 g/6 oz) green beans, chopped
1 cup (155 g/5 oz) frozen peas
1 cup (40 g/1 1/4 oz) shredded English spinach leaves
1/4 cup (15 g/1/2 oz) chopped fresh basil
grated Parmesan, for serving

1 Put the oil, pancetta, onion, garlic and celery in a large pan and stir occasionally over low heat for 8 minutes, or until the vegetables are soft but not brown. Add the stock and bring to the boil. Simmer, covered, for 10 minutes.

2 Add the macaroni and boil for 12 minutes, or until almost *al dente*. Stir in the zucchini, cabbage, beans and peas and simmer for 5 minutes. Add the spinach and basil and simmer for 2 minutes. Season to taste and serve with the grated Parmesan.

NUTRITION PER SERVE (6)
Protein 7 g; Fat 20 g; Carbohydrate 15 g; Dietary Fibre 6 g; Cholesterol 40 mg; 1030 kJ (250 cal)

Using a sharp knife, cut the pancetta into strips, then chop finely.

Chop the zucchini and finely shred the savoy cabbage.

Add the shredded spinach and basil to the soup and simmer for 2 minutes.

## ITALIAN SAUSAGE STEW

Preparation time: 15 minutes
Total cooking time: 45 minutes
Serves 4

2 large red capsicums
1 tablespoon olive oil
2 large red onions, sliced into thick
    wedges
2 cloves garlic, finely chopped
600 g (1¼ lb) Italian-style thin pork
    sausages
300 g (10 oz) can chickpeas, drained
150 g (5 oz) flat mushrooms, thickly
    sliced
½ cup (125 ml/4 fl oz) dry white wine
2 bay leaves
2 teaspoons chopped fresh rosemary
400 g (13 oz) can diced tomatoes

**1** Cut the capsicums into large pieces, removing the seeds and membrane. Place skin-side-up, under a hot grill until the skin blackens and blisters. Allow to cool in a plastic bag. Peel away the skin, and slice diagonally into thick strips.
**2** Meanwhile, heat the oil in a non-stick frying pan. Add the onion and garlic, and stir over medium heat for 6 minutes, or until the onion is soft and browned. Remove the onion from the pan. Add the sausages to the same pan. Cook over medium heat, turning occasionally, for 8 minutes, or until the sausages are browned. Remove the sausages and slice diagonally into 3 cm (1¼ inch) pieces.
**3** Combine the capsicum, onion, sausage, chickpeas and mushrooms in the pan and cook over medium–high heat for 5 minutes.

**4** Add the wine, bay leaves and rosemary. Bring to the boil, then reduce the heat to low and simmer for 3 minutes. Stir in the tomatoes and simmer for 20 minutes, or until the sauce has thickened slightly. Remove the bay leaves and season to taste with sugar, salt and cracked black pepper. Delicious served with fettucine, noodles, grilled ciabatta bread, mashed potato, soft polenta, or Parmesan shavings.

NUTRITION PER SERVE
Protein 20 g; Fat 25 g; Carbohydrate 25 g; Dietary Fibre 9.5 g; Cholesterol 50 mg; 1695 kJ (405 Cal)

STORAGE TIME: This stew can be stored in the refrigerator for up to 2 days.

Grill the capsicums under a hot grill until the skin blackens and blisters.

Remove the skin from the cooled capsicums and slice them into thin strips.

Use a pair of tongs to hold the sausages as you slice them into 3 cm (¼ inch) pieces.

## PASTA E FAGIOLI (HEARTY PASTA AND BEAN SOUP)

Preparation time: 15 minutes
Total cooking time: 20 minutes
Serves 4

1 tablespoon olive oil
1 onion, finely chopped
3 cloves garlic, crushed
2 x 290 g (10 oz) cans mixed beans,
    drained
1.75 litres chicken stock (see NOTE)
100 g (3½ oz) conchigliette
1 tablespoon chopped fresh tarragon

**1** Heat the oil in a saucepan over low heat. Add the onion and cook for 5 minutes, then add the garlic and cook for a further 1 minute, stirring frequently. Add the beans and chicken stock, cover the pan with a lid, increase the heat and bring to the boil.
**2** Add the pasta and cook until *al dente*. Stir in the tarragon, then season with salt and cracked black pepper. Serve accompanied by crusty bread.

NUTRITION PER SERVE
Protein 12 g; Fat 6.5 g; Carbohydrate 34 g;
Dietary Fibre 8 g; Cholesterol 0 mg; 1015 kJ
(240 Cal)

NOTE: The flavour of this soup is really enhanced by using a good-quality stock. Either make your own or use the tetra packs of liquid stock that are available at the supermarket.

Add the beans and the chicken stock to the pan.

# pasta & gnocchi

## PASTA POMODORO

Preparation time: 15 minutes
Total cooking time: 10–15 minutes
Serves 4

500 g (1 lb) pasta
1½ tablespoons olive oil
1 onion, very finely chopped
2 x 400 g (13 oz) cans Italian
   tomatoes, chopped
¼ cup (7 g/¼ oz) fresh basil leaves

**1** Cook the pasta in a large pan of rapidly boiling salted water until *al dente*. Drain and return to the pan to keep warm.
**2** Heat the oil in a large frying pan.

Add the onion and cook over medium heat until softened. Stir in the chopped tomato and simmer for 5–6 minutes, or until the sauce has reduced slightly and thickened. Season with salt and freshly ground pepper. Stir in the basil leaves and cook for another minute.

To finely chop an onion, cut it in half and slice horizontally, without cutting all the way through.

**3** Pour the sauce over the warm pasta and gently toss. Serve immediately.

NUTRITION PER SERVE:
Protein 20 g; Fat 10 g; Carbohydrate 95 g; Dietary Fibre 10 g; Cholesterol 5 mg; 2295 kJ (545 cal)

Then make cuts close together across one way, then in the opposite direction, to make dice.

# PASTA BOSCAIOLA

Preparation time: 15 minutes
Total cooking time: 25 minutes
Serves 4

500 g (1 lb) pasta
1 tablespoon olive oil
6 bacon rashers, chopped
200 g (6¹/₂ oz) button mushrooms, sliced
2¹/₂ cups (625 ml/21 fl oz) cream
2 spring onions, sliced
1 tablespoon chopped fresh parsley

**1** Cook the pasta in a large pan of rapidly boiling salted water until *al dente*. Drain well and return to the pan to keep warm.
**2** Meanwhile, heat the oil in a large frying pan, add the bacon and mushrooms and cook, stirring, for 5 minutes, or until golden brown.
**3** Add a little of the cream and stir well with a wooden spoon.
**4** Add the remaining cream, bring to the boil and cook over high heat for 15 minutes, or until thick enough to coat the back of a spoon. Add the spring onion. Pour the sauce over the pasta and toss well. Serve sprinkled with the parsley.

NUTRITION PER SERVE
Protein 30 g; Fat 60 g; Carbohydrate 95 g; Dietary Fibre 8 g; Cholesterol 200 mg; 4310 kJ (1025 cal)

NOTE: This sauce is normally served with spaghetti, but you can use any pasta. We have shown it with casereccie. If you are short on time and don't have 15 minutes to reduce the sauce, it can be thickened with 2 teaspoons of cornflour mixed with 1 tablespoon of water. Stir until the mixture boils and thickens. 'Boscaiola' means woodcutter—collecting mushrooms is part of the heritage of the woodcutters.

Add a little of the cream and scrape the bottom of the pan with a wooden spoon.

Cook the sauce over high heat until it is thick enough to coat the back of a wooden spoon.

## PASTA WITH PESTO

Preparation time: 10–15 minutes
Total cooking time: 15 minutes
Serves 4–6

500 g (1 lb) pasta
3 tablespoons pine nuts
2 cups (100 g/3¹/2 oz) fresh basil
    leaves
2 cloves garlic, peeled
¹/2 teaspoon salt
3 tablespoons grated Parmesan
2 tablespoons grated Pecorino
    cheese, optional
¹/2 cup (125 ml/4 fl oz) olive oil

**1** Cook the pasta in a large pan of rapidly boiling salted water until *al dente*. Drain well and return to the pan to keep warm.
**2** Meanwhile, toast the pine nuts in a dry heavy-based pan over low heat for 2–3 minutes, or until golden. Allow to cool. Process the pine nuts, basil leaves, garlic, salt and cheeses in a food processor for 20 seconds, or until finely chopped.
**3** With the motor running, gradually add the oil in a thin steady stream until a paste is formed. Add freshly ground black pepper, to taste. Toss the sauce with the warm pasta until the pasta is well coated.

NUTRITION PER SERVE (6)
Protein 15 g; Fat 30 g; Carbohydrate 60 g;
Dietary Fibre 5 g; Cholesterol 8 mg;
2280 kJ (540 cal)

NOTE: Traditionally, linguine, as shown, is used with pesto but you can serve it with any pasta of your choice. Pesto sauce can be made up to one week in advance and refrigerated in an airtight container. Ensure the pesto is tightly packed and seal the surface with some plastic wrap or pour a little extra oil over the top to prevent the pesto turning black. Each time you use the pesto reseal the surface with a little oil.

Process the pine nuts, basil leaves, garlic, salt and cheeses for about 20 seconds.

With the motor running, add the olive oil in a thin steady stream, until a paste is formed.

# SPAGHETTI BOLOGNESE

Preparation time: 30 minutes
Total cooking time: 1 hour 20 minutes
Serves 6

cooking oil spray
2 onions, finely chopped
2 cloves garlic, finely chopped
2 carrots, finely chopped
2 celery sticks, finely chopped
400 g (13 oz) lean beef mince
1 kg (2 lb) tomatoes, chopped
1/2 cup (125 ml/4 fl oz) red wine

350 g (11 oz) spaghetti
1/4 cup (15 g/1/2 oz) finely chopped
  fresh parsley

**1**  Lightly spray a large saucepan with oil. Place over medium heat and add the onion, garlic, carrot and celery. Stir for 5 minutes, or until the vegetables have softened. Add 1 tablespoon water, if necessary, to prevent sticking.
**2**  Increase the heat to high, add the mince and cook for 5 minutes, or until browned. Stir constantly to prevent the meat sticking. Add the tomato, wine and 1 cup (250 ml/8 fl oz) water. Bring

to the boil, then reduce the heat and simmer, uncovered, for about 1 hour, until the sauce has thickened.
**3**  Cook the spaghetti in a large pan of rapidly boiling salted water for 10–12 minutes, or until *al dente*, then drain. Stir the parsley through the sauce, season with salt and black pepper, and serve over the pasta.

NUTRITION PER SERVE
Protein 9 g; Fat 8 g; Carbohydrate 50 g;
Dietary Fibre 7 g; Cholesterol 0 mg;
1695 kJ (405 Cal)

Finely chop both the onions and then fry with the garlic, carrot and celery.

Stir the meat constantly and break up any lumps with the back of the spoon.

Simmer the Bolognese sauce, uncovered, until the liquid has reduced and the sauce thickened.

## PROSCIUTTO AND SWEET POTATO PENNE

Preparation time: 10 minutes
Total cooking time: 15 minutes
Serves 4

500 g (1 lb) penne
500 g (1 lb) orange sweet potato, diced
2 tablespoons extra virgin olive oil
5 spring onions, sliced
2 small cloves garlic, crushed
8 thin slices prosciutto, chopped
125 g (4 oz) sun-dried tomatoes in oil, drained and sliced
1/4 cup (15 g/1/2 oz) shredded fresh basil leaves

**1** Cook the penne in a large pan of rapidly boiling salted water until *al dente*. Drain well and return to the pan to keep warm.

**2** Meanwhile, steam the sweet potato for 5 minutes, or until tender. Heat the oil in a saucepan, add the spring onion, garlic and sweet potato and stir over medium heat for 2–3 minutes, or until the spring onion is soft. Add the prosciutto and tomato and cook for a further 1 minute.

**3** Add the sweet potato mixture to the penne and toss over low heat until heated through. Add the basil and season with black pepper. Serve immediately with crusty bread.

NUTRITION PER SERVE
Protein 20 g; Fat 20 g; Carbohydrate 115 g; Dietary Fibre 11 g; Cholesterol 5 mg; 3065 kJ (732 cal)

NOTE: Orange sweet potato is also known as kumera.

Cook the spring onion, garlic and sweet potato for 2–3 minutes.

Add the sweet potato mixture to the cooked pasta and heat through.

# FETTUCINE CARBONARA

Preparation time: 10 minutes
Total cooking time: 25 minutes
Serves 4

500 g (1 lb) fettucine
3 eggs, lightly beaten
½ cup (125 ml/4 oz) cream
⅓ cup (35 g/1¼ oz) finely grated
    Parmesan
20 g (¾ oz) butter
250 g (8 oz) bacon, rind removed,
    cut into thin strips
2 cloves garlic, crushed
4 spring onions, finely chopped

**1** Bring a large pan of water to the boil, add the fettucine and cook for 10–12 minutes, or until just tender.
**2** Whisk together the eggs, cream and Parmesan and season generously.

**3** Meanwhile, melt the butter in a frying pan, add the bacon strips and cook for 5–8 minutes, or until lightly golden. Add the garlic and spring onion and cook for 2–3 minutes more. Remove from the heat.
**4** Drain the pasta, and transfer to a large serving bowl. While the pasta is still hot pour in the egg mixture and toss well to combine (the heat from the pasta should be sufficient to cook the egg). Add the bacon mixture and toss through the pasta. Season to taste with cracked black pepper and serve immediately.

NUTRITION PER SERVE
Protein 35 g; Fat 30 g; Carbohydrate 90 g;
Dietary Fibre 6.5 g; Cholesterol 235 mg;
3213 kJ (765 Cal)

Whisk together the eggs, cream, cheese, salt and pepper.

Pour the egg mixture over the hot pasta and toss to combine.

# PASTA ALFREDO

Preparation time: 10 minutes
Total cooking time: 15 minutes
Serves 4–6

500 g (1 lb) pasta (see NOTE)
90 g (3 oz) butter
1¹⁄₂ cups (150 g/5 oz) freshly
    grated Parmesan
1¹⁄₄ cups (315 ml/10 fl oz) cream
3 tablespoons chopped
    fresh parsley

**1** Cook the pasta in a large pan of rapidly boiling salted water until *al dente*. Drain and return to the pan.
**2** While the pasta is cooking, melt the butter in a pan over low heat. Add the Parmesan and cream and bring to the boil, stirring constantly. Reduce the heat and simmer, stirring, until the sauce has thickened slightly. Add the parsley and salt and pepper, to taste, and stir until well combined.
**3** Add the sauce to the pasta and toss well so the sauce coats the pasta. Garnish with chopped herbs or sprigs of fresh herbs such as thyme.

NUTRITION PER SERVE (6):
Protein 20 g; Fat 40 g; Carbohydrate 60 g;
Dietary Fibre 4 g; Cholesterol 125 mg;
2875 kJ (685 cal)

NOTE: Traditionally fettucine is used with this sauce, but you can try any pasta. Try to time the sauce so it is ready just as the pasta is cooked.

It is best to use a block of Parmesan and grate your own each time you need it.

To chop parsley, use a large sharp knife. A swivel action is easiest, holding the point of the knife.

# SPAGHETTI MARINARA

Preparation time: 40 minutes
Total cooking time: 50 minutes
Serves 6

TOMATO SAUCE
2 tablespoons olive oil
1 onion, finely chopped
1 carrot, sliced
2 cloves garlic, crushed
425 g (14 oz) can crushed tomatoes
1/2 cup (125 ml/4 fl oz) white wine
1 teaspoon sugar

20 black mussels
1/4 cup (60 ml/2 fl oz) white wine
1/4 cup (60 ml/2 fl oz) fish stock
1 clove garlic, crushed
375 g (12 oz) spaghetti
30 g (1 oz) butter
125 g (4 oz) calamari rings
125 g (4 oz) skinless firm white
    fish fillets, cubed
200 g (6 1/2 oz) raw medium prawns,
    peeled and deveined
10 g (1/4 oz) fresh flat-leaf parsley,
    chopped
200 g (6 1/2 oz) can clams, drained

**1** For the sauce, heat the oil in a deep frying pan, add the onion and carrot and stir over medium heat for 10 minutes, or until the vegetables are golden. Add the garlic, tomato, wine and sugar and bring to the boil. Reduce the heat and gently simmer for 30 minutes, stirring occasionally.
**2** Scrub the mussels and pull out the hairy beards. Discard any broken ones, or open ones that don't close when tapped. Rinse well. Heat the wine with the stock and garlic in a large frying pan. Add the mussels. Cover and shake the pan over high heat for 4–5 minutes. After 3 minutes, start removing the opened mussels. After 5 minutes, discard any unopened mussels. Reserve the liquid.
**3** Cook the spaghetti in a large pan of rapidly boiling salted water for 12 minutes, or until *al dente*. Drain.
**4** Meanwhile, melt the butter in a frying pan, add the calamari, fish and prawns in batches and stir-fry for 2 minutes, or until just cooked through. Add the seafood to the

tomato sauce with the reserved liquid, mussels, parsley and clams. Stir until the seafood is heated through. Add the spaghetti to the pan and toss well.

NUTRITION PER SERVE
Protein 34.5 g; Fat 14 g; Carbohydrate 51.5 g; Dietary Fibre 5 g; Cholesterol 139 mg; 2090 kJ (495 Cal)

SUGGESTED FISH: Blue-eye, groper, striped marlin.

NOTE: Buy the seafood and prepare your own marinara mix, rather than buying prepared marinara mixes.

Stir-fry the calamari rings, fish and prawns until just cooked through.

After adding the seafood and liquid to the sauce, stir until heated through.

# PASTA PRIMAVERA

Preparation time: 25 minutes
Total cooking time: 10–15 minutes
Serves 4

500 g (1 lb) pasta (see NOTE)
1 cup (155 g/5 oz) frozen broad beans
200 g (6¹/2 oz) sugar snap peas
155 g (5 oz) asparagus spears
30 g (1 oz) butter
1 cup (250 ml/8 fl oz) cream
60 g (2 oz) freshly grated Parmesan

**1** Cook the pasta in a large pan of rapidly boiling salted water until *al dente*. Drain and return to the pan to keep warm.
**2** Cook the beans in a pan of boiling water for 2 minutes. Plunge them into iced water and then drain. Remove and discard the skins from the broad beans—you can usually just squeeze them out, otherwise carefully slit the skins first.
**3** Trim the stalks from the peas and break the woody ends from the asparagus spears. Cut the asparagus into short lengths.
**4** Melt the butter in a heavy-based frying pan. Add the vegetables, cream and Parmesan. Simmer gently over medium heat for 3–4 minutes, or until the peas and asparagus are bright green and just tender. Season with some salt and pepper. Pour the sauce over the warm pasta and toss to combine. Serve immediately.

NUTRITION PER SERVE
Protein 30 g; Fat 35 g; Carbohydrate 95 g;
Dietary Fibre 12 g; Cholesterol 105 mg;
3420 kJ (815 cal)

NOTE: Traditionally, primavera is served with spaghetti. Here it is shown with spaghettini, a thin spaghetti.

After cooking, the broad beans should slip easily out of their skins.

Trim the stalks from the sugar snap peas and snap the woody ends from the asparagus.

# POTATO GNOCCHI WITH TOMATO SAUCE

Preparation time: 1 hour
Total cooking time: 45 minutes
Serves 4

500 g (1 lb) floury potatoes, unpeeled
1 egg yolk
3 tablespoons grated Parmesan
1 cup (125 g/4 oz) plain flour

TOMATO SAUCE
425 g (14 oz) can tomatoes
1 small onion, chopped
1 celery stick, chopped
1 small carrot, chopped
1 tablespoon shredded fresh basil
1 teaspoon chopped fresh thyme
1 clove garlic, crushed
1 teaspoon caster sugar

**1** Steam or boil the potatoes until just tender. Drain thoroughly and allow to cool for 10 minutes before peeling and mashing them.
**2** Measure 2 cups (460 g/4 oz) of the mashed potato into a large bowl. Mix in the egg yolk, Parmesan, 1/4 teaspoon of salt and some black pepper. Slowly add flour until you have a slightly sticky dough. Knead for 5 minutes, adding more flour if necessary, until a smooth dough is formed.
**3** Divide the dough into four portions and roll each portion on a lightly floured surface to form a sausage shape, about 2 cm (3/4 inch) thick.
**4** Cut the rolls into 2.5 cm (1 inch) slices and shape each piece into an oval. Press each oval into the palm of your hand against a floured fork, to flatten slightly and indent one side with a pattern. As you make the

gnocchi place them in a single layer on a baking tray and cover until ready to use.
**5** To make the tomato sauce, mix all the ingredients with salt and pepper in a pan. Bring to the boil, reduce the heat to medium–low and simmer for 30 minutes, stirring occasionally. Allow to cool, then process in a food processor or blender, until smooth. Reheat if necessary before serving.
**6** Cook the gnocchi in batches in a large pan of boiling salted water for 2 minutes, or until the gnocchi float to the surface. Drain well. Serve the gnocchi tossed through the sauce.

NUTRITION PER SERVE
Protein 10 g; Fat 4 g; Carbohydrate 45 g; Dietary Fibre 5 g; Cholesterol 50 mg; 1125 kJ (270 Cal)

NOTES: The gnocchi can be prepared several hours in advance and arranged on a tray in a single layer to prevent them sticking together. Cover and keep refrigerated. Gnocchi was traditionally made using potatoes baked in their skins. This results in a drier dough that is easy to work with, so if you have time you can use this method.

Slowly add flour to the potato mixture, until a slightly sticky dough is formed.

Knead the dough for about 5 minutes or until smooth, adding flour if necessary.

Roll each portion into a sausage shape, on a lightly floured surface.

Press each oval with a floured fork to flatten slightly and make an indentation.

Put all the ingredients for the sauce in a pan and season with salt and pepper.

Cook the gnocchi in a large pan of boiling water until they float to the surface.

## PASTA NAPOLITANA

Preparation time: 20 minutes
Total cooking time: 1 hour
Serves 4–6

2 tablespoons olive oil
1 onion, finely chopped
1 carrot, finely chopped
1 celery stick, finely chopped
500 g (1 lb) very ripe tomatoes,
    chopped
2 tablespoons chopped fresh parsley
2 teaspoons sugar
500 g (1 lb) pasta (see NOTE)

**1** Heat the oil in a heavy-based pan.
Add the onion, carrot and celery,
cover and cook for 10 minutes over
low heat, stirring occasionally.
**2** Add the tomato, parsley, sugar and
1/2 cup (125 ml/4 fl oz) of water. Bring
to the boil, reduce the heat to low,
cover and simmer for 45 minutes,
stirring occasionally. Season. If
necessary, add up to 3/4 cup (185 ml/
6 fl oz) more water.
**3** About 15 minutes before serving,
cook the pasta in a large pan of rapidly
boiling salted water until *al dente*.
Drain and return to the pan. Pour the
sauce over the pasta and gently toss.

NUTRITION PER SERVE (6):
Protein 10 g; Fat 7 g; Carbohydrate 65 g;
Dietary Fibre 6 g; Cholesterol 0 mg;
1540 kJ (365 cal)

NOTE: Traditionally, spaghetti is
served with this sauce, but you can
use any pasta. We have shown
penne rigate.

HINT: The sauce can be reduced to a
more concentrated version by
cooking it uncovered so the moisture
evaporates, for a longer period. Store it
in the refrigerator and add water or
stock to thin it, if necessary, when you
are reheating.

Dice the vegetables quite finely before cooking in
the hot oil.

The tomatoes should be very ripe to give this
sauce the best flavour.

# SPAGHETTI WITH HERB, GARLIC AND CHILLI OIL

Preparation time: 15 minutes
Total cooking time: 15 minutes
Serves 4–6

1 cup (250 ml/8 fl oz) olive oil
2 bird's eye chillies, seeded and thinly
   sliced
5–6 large cloves garlic, crushed
500 g (1 lb) spaghetti
100 g (3½ oz) thinly sliced prosciutto
½ cup (30 g/1 oz) chopped fresh flat-
   leaf parsley

2 tablespoons chopped fresh basil
2 tablespoons chopped fresh oregano
¾ cup (75 g/2½ oz) grated
   Parmesan

**1** Pour the oil into a small saucepan with the chilli and garlic. Slowly heat the oil over low heat for about 12 minutes to infuse the oil with the garlic and chilli. Don't allow the oil to reach smoking point or the garlic will burn and taste bitter.
**2** Meanwhile, cook the pasta in a large pan of rapidly boiling salted water until *al dente*. Drain well and return to the pan to keep warm. Cook

the prosciutto under a hot grill for 2 minutes each side, or until crispy. Cool and break into pieces.
**3** Pour the hot oil mixture over the spaghetti and toss well with the prosciutto, fresh herbs and Parmesan. Season to taste.

NUTRITION PER SERVE (6)
Protein 18 g; Fat 44 g; Carbohydrate 60 g;
Dietary Fibre 6 g; Cholesterol 21 mg;
2945 kJ (705 cal)

NOTE: This sauce is traditionally served with spaghetti. It is simple but relies on good-quality ingredients.

Slowly heat the oil, chilli and garlic over low heat to infuse the oil with the flavours.

Grill the prosciutto until it is crispy, then cool and break into pieces.

Pour the hot oil mixture over the drained pasta and toss well.

# PASTA WITH CLAMS

Preparation time: 25 minutes +
  overnight soaking
Total cooking time: 20 minutes
Serves 4

2 tablespoons salt
2 tablespoons plain flour
1 kg (2 lb) clams or pipis
500 g (1 lb) shell pasta
1 tablespoon olive oil
2 cloves garlic, crushed
2 x 425 g (14 oz) cans crushed
  tomatoes
1/4 cup (60 ml/2 fl oz) red wine
2 tablespoons chopped fresh parsley
1 teaspoon sugar

**1** Blend the salt and plain flour with
enough water to make a paste. Add to
a large pan of cold water and soak the
shellfish overnight. This will draw out
sand from inside the shells. Scrub the
shells well. Rinse and drain.
**2** Cook the pasta in a large pan of
rapidly boiling salted water until
*al dente*. Drain and return to the pan
to keep warm. Meanwhile, heat the oil
in a large pan. Add the garlic and cook
over low heat for 30 seconds. Add the
tomatoes, wine, parsley and sugar and
season. Stir and bring to the boil.
Reduce the heat and simmer, stirring
occasionally, for 5 minutes.
**3** Add the clams to the sauce and
cook for 3–5 minutes, stirring
occasionally, until opened. Discard
any clams that do not open in the
cooking time. Serve over the pasta.

NUTRITION PER SERVE
Protein 35 g; Fat 25 g; Carbohydrate 55 g;
Dietary Fibre 7 g; Cholesterol 355 mg;
2420 kJ (580 cal)

Cook the pasta in a large pan of rapidly boiling water until *al dente*.

Add the tomatoes, wine, parsley and sugar and stir well.

Add the scrubbed clams or pipis to the sauce and cook until they open.

# BLUE CHEESE GNOCCHI

Preparation time: 20 minutes
Total cooking time: 20 minutes
Serves 4

500 g (1 lb) potatoes, quartered
1¼ cups (155 g/5 oz) plain flour

SAUCE
300 ml (10 fl oz) cream
125 g (4 oz) Gorgonzola cheese,
    roughly chopped
2 tablespoons chopped fresh chives

**1**  Cook the potatoes in boiling salted water for 15–20 minutes or in the microwave until tender. Stir through a generous amount of salt. Drain the potatoes, then mash until completely smooth. Transfer to a bowl.

**2**  Sprinkle the flour into the bowl with one hand while kneading it into the potato mixture with the other hand. Continue kneading until all the flour is worked in and the dough is smooth. This should take a few minutes and will be sticky at first.

**3**  Divide the dough into three and roll each portion into a sausage that is 2 cm (¾ inch) thick. Cut into 2.5 cm (1 inch) lengths and, using floured hands, press each gnocchi against a fork to flatten it and indent one side (the indentation helps the sauce coat the gnocchi).

**4**  Bring a large pan of water to the boil. Drop in the gnocchi, then reduce the heat and simmer until they rise to the surface. This will take 2–3 minutes. Lift out of the water with a slotted spoon and drain well. Arrange on a warm serving dish and keep warm.

**5**  Put the cream into a small pan and bring to the boil. Boil rapidly, stirring constantly, for about 5 minutes, or until reduced by one third. Remove from the heat and stir in the cheese. Season with salt and pepper, and pour over the gnocchi. Scatter the chives over the top and serve immediately.

NUTRITION PER SERVE (8)
Protein 5 g; Fat 11 g; Carbohydrate 11 g;
Dietary Fibre 0.5 g; Cholesterol 30 mg;
680 kJ (165 Cal)

Add the flour with one hand while kneading it into the potato with the other.

Gently knead the mixture until all the flour is mixed in and the dough is smooth.

Press the gnocchi against a fork to flatten it and indent one side.

Drop the gnocchi into boiling water and simmer until they rise.

# FETTUCINE WITH CHICKEN AND MUSHROOM SAUCE

Preparation time: 10 minutes
Total cooking time: 25 minutes
Serves 4

2 (330 g/11 oz) chicken breast fillets
1 tablespoon olive oil
30 g (1 oz) butter
2 slices bacon, cut into thin strips
2 cloves garlic, crushed
250 g (8 oz) button mushrooms, sliced
1/3 cup (80 ml/2³/4 fl oz) dry white wine
2/3 cup (170 ml/5¹/2 fl oz) cream
4 spring onions, chopped
1 tablespoon plain flour
400 g (13 oz) fettucine
1/3 cup (35 g/1¹/4 oz) grated
 Parmesan

**1** Trim the chicken of excess fat and sinew, and cut into thin strips. Heat the oil and butter in a heavy-based frying pan. Add the chicken and cook over medium heat for 3 minutes, or until browned.
**2** Add the bacon, garlic and mushrooms, and cook over medium heat for 2 minutes, stirring occasionally.
**3** Add the wine and cook until the liquid has reduced by half. Add the cream and spring onion, and bring to the boil. Blend the flour with 2 tablespoons water until smooth. Add to the pan and stir over the heat until the mixture boils and thickens, then reduce the heat and simmer for 2 minutes. Season to taste.
**4** Cook the fettucine in a large pan of rapidly boiling water with a little oil added, then drain. Add the fettucine to the sauce and stir over low heat until combined. Sprinkle with Parmesan and serve immediately with a green salad and herb bread.

NUTRITION PER SERVE
Protein 40 g; Fat 35 g; Carbohydrate 75 g;
Dietary Fibre 7 g; Cholesterol 136 mg;
3380 kJ (808 cal)

Trim the chicken of excess fat and sinew, and cut into thin strips.

Add the bacon, garlic and mushrooms to the chicken and cook over medium heat.

Add the cream and spring onion to the pan and bring to the boil.

Add the fettucine to the sauce and stir over low heat until combined.

# ZITI WITH SAUSAGE

Preparation time: 10 minutes
Total cooking time: 35 minutes
Serves 4

1 red capsicum
1 green capsicum
1 small eggplant, sliced
3 tablespoons olive oil
1 onion, sliced
1 clove garlic, crushed
250 g (8 oz) chipolata sausages, sliced
425 g (14 oz) can crushed tomatoes
1/2 cup (125 ml/4 fl oz) red wine
3 tablespoons halved pitted black
   olives
1 tablespoon chopped fresh basil
1 tablespoon chopped fresh parsley
500 g (1 lb) ziti
2 tablespoons grated Parmesan, for
   serving

**1** Cut both capsicums into large flat pieces, removing the seeds and membranes. Place under a hot grill until the skin blackens and blisters. Cover with a damp tea towel and then peel off the skin. Chop and set aside.
**2** Brush the eggplant with a little oil. Grill until golden on each side, brushing with more oil as required. Set aside.
**3** Heat the remaining oil in a frying pan. Add the onion and garlic and stir over low heat until the onion is tender. Add the chipolatas and cook until well browned.
**4** Stir in the tomatoes, wine, olives, basil, parsley and salt and pepper. Bring to the boil. Reduce the heat and simmer for 15 minutes. Add the vegetables and heat through. Meanwhile, cook the ziti in a large pan of rapidly boiling salted water until *al dente*. Drain well and return to the pan to keep warm. Toss the vegetables and sauce through the hot pasta. Sprinkle with Parmesan cheese before serving.

NUTRITION PER SERVE
Protein 19 g; Fat 19 g; Carbohydrate 97 g;
Dietary Fibre 11 g; Cholesterol 5 mg;
2756 kJ (650 cal)

NOTE: Ziti is a wide tubular pasta.
You could use fettucine or spaghetti.

Grill the capsicums to remove the skins and then chop the flesh.

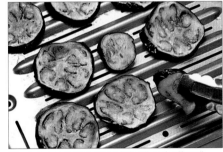
Brush the eggplant with a little oil and grill until golden on both sides.

Cook the onion until it is tender and then add the sliced chipolatas.

Drain the pasta and return to the pan, then add the hot sauce and toss well.

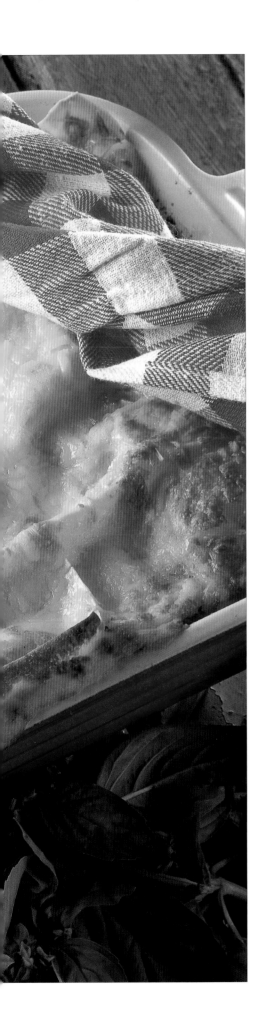

# CLASSIC LASAGNE

Preparation time: 25 minutes
Total cooking time: 1 hour 15 minutes
Serves 4–6

250 g (8 oz) lasagne sheets
1/2 cup (75 g/11/2 oz) grated
    mozzarella
1/2 cup (60 g/2 oz) grated Cheddar
1/2 cup (125 ml/4 fl oz) cream
3 tablespoons grated Parmesan

CHEESE SAUCE
60 g (2 oz) butter
1/3 cup (40 g/11/4 oz) plain flour
2 cups (500 ml/16 fl oz) milk
1 cup (125 g/4 oz) grated Cheddar

MEAT SAUCE
1 tablespoon olive oil
1 onion, finely chopped
1 clove garlic, crushed
500 g (1 lb) beef mince
2 x 425 g (14 oz) cans tomatoes
1/4 cup (60 ml/2 fl oz) red wine
1/2 teaspoon ground oregano
1/4 teaspoon ground basil

**1** Preheat the oven to moderate 180°C (350°F/Gas 4). Brush a shallow oven-proof dish (approximately 24 x 30 cm /10 x 12 inches) with melted butter or oil. Line with lasagne sheets, breaking them to fill any gaps, and set aside.
**2** To make the cheese sauce, melt the butter in a pan. Add the flour and stir for 1 minute. Remove from the heat and slowly add the milk, stirring until smooth. Return to the heat and cook, stirring, over medium heat until the sauce boils and thickens. Reduce the heat and simmer for 3 minutes. Stir in the cheese, season and set aside.
**3** To make the meat sauce, heat the oil in a large pan. Add the onion and garlic and stir over low heat until the onion is tender. Add the mince and brown well, breaking up with a fork as it cooks. Stir in the tomatoes, wine, oregano, basil and salt and pepper. Bring to the boil, reduce the heat and simmer for 20 minutes.
**4** Spoon one-third of the meat sauce over the lasagne sheets. Top with one-third of the cheese sauce. Arrange another layer of lasagne sheets over the top.
**5** Continue layering, finishing with lasagne sheets. Sprinkle with the combined mozzarella and Cheddar cheeses. Pour the cream over the top. Sprinkle with Parmesan. Bake for 35–40 minutes or until golden.

NUTRITION PER SERVE (6)
Protein 41 g; Fat 58 g; Carbohydrate 45 g; Dietary Fibre 5 g; Cholesterol 170 mg; 3765 kJ (899 cal)

NOTE: Cheese sauce is a variation of Béchamel sauce that uses milk infused with flavourings such as bay leaf, cloves, peppercorns, parsley sprig and cinnamon stick. To do this, bring milk to boiling point with one or more of the flavourings and allow to stand for 10 minutes before straining for the flavours to infuse.

Arrange a layer of lasagne sheets in the base of the ovenproof dish.

Spread a layer of meat sauce over the lasagne sheets and then build up the layers.

## LINGUINE WITH HAM, ARTICHOKE AND LEMON SAUCE

Preparation time: 15 minutes
Total cooking time: 10 minutes
Serves 4

500 g (1 lb) fresh linguine
1 tablespoon butter
2 large cloves garlic, chopped
150 g (5 oz) marinated artichokes, drained and quartered
150 g (5 oz) sliced leg ham, cut into strips
300 ml (10 fl oz) cream
2 teaspoons roughly grated lemon rind
1/2 cup (15 g/1/2 oz) fresh basil, torn
1/3 cup (35 g/1 oz) grated Parmesan

**1** Cook the pasta in a large pan of rapidly boiling salted water until *al dente*. Drain and return to the pan to keep warm. Meanwhile, melt the butter in a large frying pan, add the garlic and cook over medium heat for 1 minute, or until fragrant. Add the artichokes and ham and cook for a further 2 minutes.

**2** Add the cream and lemon rind, reduce the heat and simmer for 5 minutes, gently breaking up the artichokes with a wooden spoon. Pour the sauce over the pasta, then add the basil and Parmesan and toss well until the pasta is evenly coated. Serve immediately.

NUTRITION PER SERVE
Protein 26 g; Fat 42 g; Carbohydrate 91 g;
Dietary Fibre 8 g; Cholesterol 143 mg;
3540 kJ (845 cal)

Add the artichokes and ham to the frying pan and cook for 2 minutes.

Add the cream and lemon rind, reduce the heat and simmer for 5 minutes.

# PASTA ARRABBIATA

Preparation time: 30 minutes
Total cooking time: 50 minutes
Serves 4

1/2 cup (75 g/2 1/2 oz) bacon fat
2–3 fresh red chillies
2 tablespoons olive oil
1 large onion, finely chopped
1 clove garlic, finely chopped
500 g (1 lb) very ripe tomatoes,
    finely chopped
500 g (1 lb) pasta
2 tablespoons chopped fresh parsley
grated Parmesan or Pecorino cheese,
    for serving

**1** Use a large knife to finely chop the bacon fat. Chop the chillies, taking care to avoid skin irritation—wearing rubber gloves will help. Heat the oil in a heavy-based pan and add the bacon fat, chilli, onion and garlic. Fry for 8 minutes, stirring occasionally.
**2** Add the chopped tomato to the pan with 1/2 cup (125 ml/4 fl oz) of water and season to taste. Cover and simmer for about 40 minutes, or until the sauce is thick and rich.
**3** When the sauce is almost cooked, cook the pasta in a large pan of rapidly boiling water until *al dente*. Drain well and return to the pan.
**4** Add the parsley to the sauce and toss gently with the pasta. Serve with the Parmesan or Pecorino cheese sprinkled over the top.

NUTRITION PER SERVE
Protein 20 g; Fat 25 g; Carbohydrate 95 g;
Dietary Fibre 9 g; Cholesterol 20 mg;
2880 kJ (685 cal)

NOTE: Penne rigate, as shown, is traditionally served with this sauce.

Remove the stalks and slice the chillies in half. Wear rubber gloves to protect your skin.

The chilli seeds and membrane are left in as this is a fiery sauce, but remove them if you prefer.

## SPAGHETTI WITH SALAMI AND CAPSICUM

Preparation time: 15 minutes
Total cooking time: 55 minutes
Serves 4–6

2 tablespoons olive oil
1 large onion, finely chopped
2 cloves garlic, crushed
150 g (5 oz) spicy salami slices, cut into strips
2 large red capsicums, chopped
825 g (1 lb 11 oz) can crushed tomatoes
1/2 cup (125 ml/4 fl oz) dry white wine
1 teaspoon dried basil
500 g (1 lb) spaghetti

**1** Heat the oil in a heavy-based frying pan. Add the onion, garlic and salami and cook, stirring, for 5 minutes over medium heat. Add the capsicum, cover the pan and cook for 5 minutes.
**2** Add the crushed tomatoes, wine and basil. Bring to the boil, then reduce the heat and simmer, covered, for 15 minutes.
**3** Uncover the pan and simmer for another 15 minutes, or until the sauce has thickened slightly. Season well.

**4** Meanwhile, cook the pasta in a large pan of rapidly boiling salted water until *al dente*. Drain and toss with the sauce to serve.

NUTRITION PER SERVE (6)
Protein 15 g; Fat 13 g; Carbohydrate 66 g; Dietary Fibre 6 g; Cholesterol 16 mg; 1926 kJ (460 cal)

HINT: If you can't find canned crushed tomatoes, chop whole peeled tomatoes in the can with scissors.

Cook the onion, garlic and salami for 5 minutes, then add the capsicum and cover the pan.

Simmer the sauce uncovered for 15 minutes to reduce the liquid and thicken. Season well.

Toss the drained cooked spaghetti with the sauce before serving.

# PASTA WITH CREAMY TOMATO AND BACON SAUCE

Preparation time: 10 minutes
Total cooking time: 15 minutes
Serves 4

400 g (13 oz) pasta
1 tablespoon olive oil
180 g (6 oz) streaky bacon, thinly
    sliced (see NOTE)
500 g (1 lb) Roma tomatoes, roughly
    chopped
1/2 cup (125 ml/4 fl oz) thick cream
2 tablespoons sun-dried tomato pesto
2 tablespoons finely chopped fresh
    flat-leaf parsley
1/2 cup (50 g/1³/4 oz) finely grated
    Parmesan

**1** Cook the pasta in a large pan of rapidly boiling salted water until *al dente*. Drain and return to the pan to keep warm. Meanwhile, heat the oil in a frying pan, add the bacon and cook over high heat for 2 minutes, or until starting to brown. Reduce the heat to medium, add the tomato and cook, stirring frequently, for 2 minutes, or until the tomato has softened but still holds its shape.
**2** Add the cream and tomato pesto and stir until heated through. Remove from the heat, add the parsley, then toss the sauce through the pasta with the grated Parmesan.

NUTRITION PER SERVE
Protein 25 g; Fat 29 g; Carbohydrate 75 g;
Dietary Fibre 7 g; Cholesterol 63 mg;
2745 kJ (655 cal)

NOTE: Streaky bacon is the tail fatty ends of bacon rashers and adds flavour to the dish. You can use ordinary bacon rashers if you prefer.

Cook the bacon until it is starting to brown, then add the tomato and cook until softened.

Add the cream and tomato pesto and stir until heated through.

## SPINACH AND RICOTTA GNOCCHI

Preparation time: 45 minutes +
  1 hour refrigeration
Total cooking time: 15 minutes
Serves 4

4 slices white bread
1/2 cup (125 ml/4 fl oz) milk
500 g (1 lb) frozen spinach, thawed
250 g (8 oz) ricotta cheese
2 eggs
60 g (2 oz) Parmesan, grated
1/4 cup (30 g/1 oz) plain flour
Parmesan shavings, to serve

GARLIC BUTTER SAUCE
100 g (3 1/2 oz) butter
2 cloves garlic, crushed
3 tablespoons chopped fresh basil
1 ripe tomato, diced

**1** Remove the crusts from the bread and soak in milk in a shallow dish for 10 minutes. Squeeze out any excess milk from the bread. Squeeze out any excess liquid from the spinach.
**2** Place the bread, spinach, ricotta, eggs and Parmesan in a bowl and mix thoroughly. Refrigerate, covered, for 1 hour. Fold the flour in well.
**3** Lightly dust your hands in flour and roll heaped teaspoons of the mixture into dumplings. Lower batches of the gnocchi into a large saucepan of boiling salted water. Cook for about 2 minutes, or until the gnocchi rise to the surface. Transfer to a serving plate and keep warm.
**4** To make the sauce, combine all the ingredients in a small saucepan and cook over medium heat for 3 minutes, or until the butter is nutty brown. Drizzle over the gnocchi and sprinkle with the shaved Parmesan.

NUTRITION PER SERVE
Protein 12 g; Fat 16 g; Carbohydrate 12 g;
Dietary Fibre 4 g; Cholesterol 95 mg;
1000 kJ (250 Cal)

Gently squeeze out any excess milk from the soaked bread.

With floured hands, roll teaspoons of the mixture into dumplings.

Cook the gnocchi in batches until they rise to the surface of the water.

# SMOKED SALMON PASTA

Preparation time: 10 minutes
Total cooking time: 15 minutes
Serves 4

500 g (1 lb) pasta
1 tablespoon olive oil
4 spring onions, finely chopped
180 g (6 oz) button mushrooms, sliced
1 cup (250 ml/8 fl oz) dry white wine
300 ml (10 fl oz) cream
1 tablespoon finely chopped fresh dill
1 tablespoon lemon juice

90 g (3 oz) Parmesan, grated
200 g (6½ oz) smoked salmon, cut
 into strips
shaved Parmesan and lemon wedges,
 to serve

**1** Cook the pasta in a large pan of rapidly boiling salted water until *al dente*. Drain and return to the pan to keep warm.
**2** Meanwhile, heat the oil in a small saucepan, add the spring onion and mushrooms and cook over medium heat for 1–2 minutes, or until soft. Add the wine and cream and bring to the

boil, then reduce the heat and simmer for 1 minute.
**3** Pour the mushroom sauce over the pasta and stir through the dill and lemon juice. Add the Parmesan and stir until warmed through. Remove from the heat and stir in the smoked salmon. Season with pepper and serve with Parmesan shavings and lemon wedges.

NUTRITION PER SERVE
Protein 40 g; Fat 60 g; Carbohydrate 90 g;
Dietary Fibre 8 g; Cholesterol 184 mg;
4608 kJ (1101 cal)

Cook the spring onion and mushrooms over medium heat until soft.

Add the wine and cream to the saucepan and bring to the boil.

Stir the smoked salmon through the pasta to gently warm.

# TORTELLINI WITH MUSHROOM SAUCE

Preparation time: 25 minutes
Total cooking time: 1 hour 30 minutes
Serves 4

### PASTA
2 cups (250 g/8 oz) plain flour
pinch of salt
3 eggs
1 tablespoon olive oil

### FILLING
125 g (4 oz) packet frozen spinach,
    thawed, excess liquid removed
125 g (4 oz) ricotta cheese
2 tablespoons grated Parmesan
    cheese
1 egg, beaten

### SAUCE
1 tablespoon olive oil
1 clove garlic, crushed
125 g (4 oz) mushrooms, sliced
1 cup (250 ml/8 fl oz) cream
3 tablespoons grated Parmesan
    cheese

3 tablespoons grated Parmesan
    cheese, to serve
3 tablespoons finely chopped fresh
    parsley, to serve

**1** To make the pasta, sift the flour and salt onto a board. Make a well in the centre of the flour. Whisk together the eggs, oil and 1 tablespoon water. Add this gradually to the flour, working in with your hands until the mixture forms a ball. Add a little more water if necessary. Knead on a lightly floured surface for 5 minutes or until the dough is smooth and elastic. Put in a lightly oiled bowl, cover with plastic wrap and leave for 30 minutes.

**2** To make the filling, mix together the drained spinach, ricotta, Parmesan, egg, and salt and pepper. Set aside.

**3** To make the sauce, heat the oil in a frying pan. Add the garlic and stir over low heat for 30 seconds. Add the mushrooms and cook for 3 minutes. Pour in the cream.

**4** Roll out the dough on a lightly floured surface until about 1 mm thick. Using a floured cutter, cut into 5 cm (2 inch) rounds. Spoon about 1/2 teaspoon of filling in the centre of each round. Brush a little water around the edge. Fold each round in half to form a semi-circle. Press the edges together firmly. Wrap each semi-circle around your forefinger to make a ring. Press the ends of the dough together firmly.

**5** Cook the tortellini in batches in a large pan of rapidly boiling water for about 8 minutes each batch—until the pasta is *al dente*. Drain well and return to the pan. Keep warm.

**6** Return the sauce to the heat. Bring to the boil then reduce the heat and simmer for 3 minutes. Add the Parmesan cheese and salt and pepper and stir well. Toss the sauce and tortellini together and serve immediately in warmed bowls.

**7** Mix together the Parmesan and chopped parsley and serve as an accompaniment to the pasta.

NUTRITION PER SERVE
Protein 27 g; Fat 52 g; Carbohydrate 49 g;
Dietary Fibre 5 g; Cholesterol 299 mg;
3220 kJ (770 cal)

Knead the pasta dough on a lightly floured surface until smooth and elastic.

Mix together the spinach, ricotta, Parmesan and egg to make the filling.

Fry the garlic and mushrooms and then pour in the cream to make the sauce.

Spoon a little filling into the centre of each round, then fold over and twist round your finger.

Cook the tortellini in batches so that you don't overcrowd the pan.

Reheat the sauce and then toss well with the tortellini and serve immediately.

## PASTA WITH ROASTED TOMATO SAUCE

Preparation time: 25 minutes
Total cooking time: 50 minutes
Serves 4

1 kg (2 lb) ripe Roma tomatoes
8 cloves garlic, unpeeled
2 tablespoons olive oil
2 teaspoons dried basil
1 cup (250 ml/8 fl oz) vegetable stock
1/2 cup (125 ml/4 fl oz) dry white wine
2 tablespoons balsamic vinegar
500 g (1 lb) tagliatelle
2 tablespoons grated Parmesan

**1** Preheat the oven to moderate 180°C (350°F/Gas 4). Cut the tomatoes in half lengthways and arrange, cut-side-up, in a baking dish. Sprinkle with 1 tablespoon water to prevent the tomatoes sticking. Add the garlic to the pan and drizzle or brush the oil over the tomatoes and garlic. Sprinkle with basil, salt and freshly ground black pepper. Bake for 25 minutes, or until soft, and gently remove from the pan.
**2** Heat the baking dish over low heat and add the stock, white wine and vinegar. Bring to the boil, reduce the heat and simmer for 20 minutes. Roughly chop the tomatoes, retaining all the juices. Squeeze the garlic out of

the skin and add the tomato and garlic to the simmering sauce. Taste and adjust the seasonings.
**3** Cook the pasta in a large pan of rapidly boiling salted water until *al dente*. Drain and return to the pan to keep warm. Serve the sauce over the pasta and sprinkle with Parmesan.

NUTRITION PER SERVE
Protein 20 g; Fat 3.5 g; Carbohydrate 95 g; Dietary Fibre 10 g; Cholesterol 5 mg; 2060 kJ (515 cal)

Discard the stalks of the tomatoes, then cut in half lengthways.

Add the stock, wine and vinegar to the baking dish and bring to the boil.

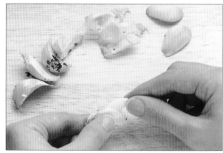

Squeeze the cooked garlic out of the skins and add to the sauce.

# SPAGHETTI WITH SHELLFISH AND WHITE WINE SAUCE

Preparation time: 15 minutes
Total cooking time: 15 minutes
Serves 4

500 g (1 lb) mussels
1 kg (2 lb) clams
400 g (13 oz) spaghetti
2 tablespoons olive oil
4 French shallots, finely chopped
2 cloves garlic, crushed
1 cup (250 ml/8 fl oz) dry white wine
3 tablespoons chopped fresh
    flat-leaf parsley

**1** Scrub the mussels with a stiff brush and remove any barnacles with a knife. Pull away the beards. Discard any mussels or clams that are broken or open ones that do not close when tapped on the work surface. Wash them both thoroughly under cold running water. Cook the pasta in a large pan of rapidly boiling salted water until *al dente*. Drain and return to the pan to keep warm.

**2** Meanwhile, heat the oil in a large saucepan over medium heat and cook the shallots for 4 minutes, or until softened. Add the garlic and cook for a further 1 minute. Pour in the wine, bring to the boil and cook for 2 minutes, or until reduced slightly. Add the clams and mussels, tossing to coat them in the liquid, then cover the pan. Cook, shaking the pan regularly, for about 3 minutes, or until the shells have opened. Discard any clams or mussels that do not open in the cooking time. Toss the clam mixture through the spaghetti, scatter with parsley and transfer to a warmed serving dish. Season and serve with salad and bread.

NUTRITION PER SERVE
Protein 37 g; Fat 12 g; Carbohydrate 76 g; Dietary Fibre 6 g; Cholesterol 68 mg; 2520 kJ (600 cal)

Scrub the mussels and then pull away the hairy beards that grow between the shells.

Cook the mussels and clams in the sauce for 3 minutes, discarding any that don't open.

## VEAL RAVIOLI WITH HERB BUTTER

Preparation time: 10 minutes
Total cooking time: 15 minutes
Serves 4

500 g (1 lb) veal ravioli
100 g (3$\frac{1}{2}$ oz) butter, softened
3 cloves garlic, crushed
2 tablespoons finely chopped fresh
    flat-leaf parsley
2 teaspoons finely chopped fresh sage
2 teaspoons chopped fresh thyme
$\frac{1}{4}$ cup (60 ml/2 fl oz) white wine
1 large vine-ripened tomato, diced

**1** Cook the pasta in a large pan of
rapidly boiling salted water until
*al dente*. Drain and return to the pan
to keep warm.

**2** Meanwhile, melt the butter in a
large frying pan over medium heat.
Add the garlic and herbs and cook,
stirring, for 1 minute. Add the wine
and cook for another minute. Pour
over the pasta, add the tomato and
toss over medium heat until warmed
through. Divide among four serving
plates and serve.

NUTRITION PER SERVE
Protein 14 g; Fat 29 g; Carbohydrate 47 g;
Dietary Fibre 6 g; Cholesterol 96 mg;
2140 kJ (510 cal)

Cook the ravioli in a large pan of rapidly boiling
water until it is tender.

Melt the butter in a frying pan and add the garlic
and herbs.

## LASAGNETTE WITH SPICY CHICKEN MEATBALLS

Preparation time: 10 minutes
Total cooking time: 15 minutes
Serves 4

750 g (1 1/2 lb) chicken mince
2 tablespoons chopped fresh
   coriander leaves
1 1/2 tablespoons red curry paste
2 tablespoons oil
1 red onion, finely chopped
3 cloves garlic, crushed
3 1/2 cups (875 g/1 lb 13 oz) tomato
   pasta sauce

2 teaspoons soft brown sugar
350 g (11 oz) lasagnette

**1** Line a tray with baking paper. Combine the mince, coriander and 1 tablespoon of the curry paste in a bowl. Roll heaped tablespoons of the mixture into balls and put on the tray—you should get about 20 balls. Refrigerate until ready to use.
**2** Heat the oil in a large deep frying pan and cook the onion and garlic over medium heat for 2–3 minutes, or until softened. Add the remaining curry paste and cook, stirring, for 1 minute, or until fragrant. Add the pasta sauce and sugar and stir well.

Reduce the heat, add the meatballs and cook, turning halfway through, for 10 minutes, or until the meatballs are cooked through.
**3** Meanwhile, cook the pasta in a large pan of rapidly boiling salted water until *al dente*. Drain and divide among four serving bowls. Top with the sauce and meatballs and sprinkle with fresh coriander to serve.

NUTRITION PER SERVE
Protein 52 g; Fat 29 g; Carbohydrate 79 g;
Dietary Fibre 8.5 g; Cholesterol 185 mg;
3300 kJ (790 cal)

Roll heaped tablespoons of the mixture into balls and place on the lined tray.

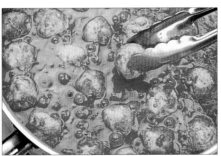

Simmer the meatballs in the sauce, turning once, until they are cooked through.

Cook the lasagnette in a large pan of boiling water until it is *al dente*.

## TAGLIATELLE WITH ASPARAGUS, PEAS AND HERB SAUCE

Preparation time: 20 minutes
Total cooking time: 25 minutes
Serves 4

375 g (12 oz) dried or 500 g (1 lb)
 fresh tagliatelle
1 cup (250 ml/8 fl oz) chicken or
 vegetable stock
2 leeks (white part only), thinly sliced
3 cloves garlic, crushed
1½ cups (235 g/7½ oz) fresh peas
1 tablespoon finely chopped fresh
 mint
400 g (13 oz) asparagus spears,
 trimmed and cut into 5 cm (2 inch)
 lengths
¼ cup (15 g/½ oz) finely chopped
 fresh parsley
½ cup (30 g/1 oz) shredded fresh
 basil
⅓ cup (80 ml/2¾ fl oz) light cream
pinch nutmeg
1 tablespoon grated fresh Parmesan
2 tablespoons extra virgin olive oil,
 to drizzle

**1** Bring a saucepan of salted water to
the boil and cook the tagliatelle until
*al dente*. Drain well.
**2** Place ½ cup (125 ml/4 fl oz) stock
and the leek in a large, deep, frying
pan. Cook over low heat, stirring
often, for 4–5 minutes. Stir in the
garlic, peas and mint and cook for
1 minute. Add the remaining stock and
½ cup (125 ml/4 fl oz) water and bring
to the boil. Simmer for 5 minutes. Add
the asparagus, parsley and basil, and
season well. Simmer for a further
3–4 minutes, or until the asparagus is
just tender. Gradually increase the heat
to reduce the sauce to a light coating
consistency. Stir in the cream, nutmeg
and Parmesan and adjust the seasoning.
**3** Toss the tagliatelle with the sauce to
coat. Drizzle each serving with olive
oil and garnish with extra grated
Parmesan, if desired.

NUTRITION PER SERVE
Protein 21 g; Fat 11 g; Carbohydrate 76 g;
Dietary Fibre 9 g; Cholesterol 32 mg;
2080 kJ (495 Cal)

Stir the garlic, peas and mint into the stock and
leek mixture.

Once the sauce has reduced, stir in the cream,
nutmeg and grated Parmesan.

## PASTA WITH ANCHOVIES, BROCCOLI AND BASIL

Preparation time: 15 minutes
Total cooking time: 25 minutes
Serves 4–6

600 g (1¼ lb) broccoli, cut into florets
500 g (1 lb) orecchiette
1 tablespoon olive oil
4 cloves garlic, finely chopped
8 anchovy fillets, roughly chopped
1 cup (250 ml/8 fl oz) cream
1 cup (30 g/1 oz) fresh basil, torn
2 teaspoons finely grated lemon rind
100 g (3½ oz) Parmesan, grated

**1** Blanch the broccoli in a large saucepan of boiling salted water for 3–4 minutes. Remove and plunge into chilled water. Drain well with a slotted spoon. Cook the pasta in a large pan of rapidly boiling salted water until *al dente*. Drain and return to the pan to keep warm, reserving 2 tablespoons of the cooking water.
**2** Meanwhile, heat the oil in a frying pan over medium heat. Add the garlic and anchovies and cook for 1–2 minutes, or until the garlic begins to turn golden. Add the broccoli and cook for a further 5 minutes. Add the cream and half the basil and cook for 10 minutes, or until the cream has

reduced and slightly thickened and the broccoli is very tender.
**3** Purée half the mixture in a food processor until nearly smooth, then return to the pan with the lemon rind, half the Parmesan and 2 tablespoons of the reserved water. Stir together well, then season. Add the warm pasta and remaining basil, and toss until well combined. Sprinkle with the remaining Parmesan and serve immediately.

NUTRITION PER SERVE (6)
Protein 23 g; Fat 28 g; Carbohydrate 61 g;
Dietary Fibre 9 g; Cholesterol 77 mg;
2455 kJ (585 cal)

Blanch the broccoli in boiling salted water, then plunge into chilled water and drain well.

Add the cream and half the basil and cook until the sauce has reduced.

Purée half the mixture and then return to the pan with the lemon rind, Parmesan and water.

## SMOKED CHICKEN LINGUINE

Preparation time: 15 minutes
Total cooking time: 20 minutes
Serves 4

1 tablespoon olive oil
1 leek, thinly sliced
3 large cloves garlic, finely chopped
1/2 cup (125 ml/4 fl oz) dry white wine
300 g (10 oz) Swiss brown
    mushrooms, sliced
2 teaspoons chopped fresh thyme
300 ml (10 fl oz) thick cream
2 smoked chicken breast fillets, thinly
    sliced (see NOTE)
350 g (11 oz) fresh linguine

**1** Heat the oil in a saucepan. Add the leek and cook, stirring, over low heat for 3–4 minutes, or until soft. Add the garlic and cook for another minute.

Pour in the wine and simmer for 2–3 minutes, or until the liquid has reduced by half.
**2** Increase the heat to medium, add the mushrooms and thyme and cook for 5 minutes, or until any excess liquid has been absorbed, then add the cream and sliced chicken. Reduce the heat and simmer for 4–5 minutes, or until the sauce has slightly thickened.
**3** Meanwhile, cook the pasta in a

large pan of rapidly boiling salted water until *al dente*. Drain and divide among serving plates. Spoon on the sauce and serve.

NUTRITION PER SERVE
Protein 33 g; Fat 40 g; Carbohydrate 53 g;
Dietary Fibre 4 g; Cholesterol 207 mg;
2990 kJ (715 cal)

NOTE: Buy smoked chicken at the deli section of good supermarkets.

Cook the leek in the oil for 3–4 minutes, or until it is soft.

Add the cream and chicken and simmer until the sauce has slightly thickened.

## FUSILLI WITH TUNA, CAPERS AND PARSLEY

Preparation time: 15 minutes
Total cooking time: 10 minutes
Serves 4

425 g (14 oz) can tuna in spring water, drained
2 tablespoons olive oil
2 cloves garlic, finely chopped
2 small red chillies, finely chopped
3 tablespoons capers (see HINT)
3 tablespoons lemon juice

1/2 cup (30 g/1 oz) finely chopped fresh parsley
375 g (12 oz) fusilli

**1** Place the tuna in a bowl and flake lightly with a fork. Combine the oil, garlic, chilli, capers, lemon juice and parsley. Pour over the tuna and mix lightly. Season well.
**2** Meanwhile, cook the pasta in a large pan of rapidly boiling salted water for 10 minutes, or until *al dente*. Reserve 1/2 cup (125 ml/4 fl oz) of the cooking water, then drain the pasta. Toss the tuna mixture through the

pasta, adding enough of the reserved water to give a moist consistency. Serve immediately.

NUTRITION PER SERVE
Protein 35 g; Fat 13 g; Carbohydrate 65 g; Dietary Fibre 5 g; Cholesterol 55 mg; 2270 kJ (545 Cal)

HINT: Generally, the smaller the caper the tastier, so use baby ones if you can find them.

Finely chop the chillies. Remove the seeds if you prefer a milder taste.

Break the tuna into flakes with a fork and then mix with the dressing.

Cook the pasta in a large pan of rapidly boiling salted water.

## CREAMY VEAL AND MUSHROOM PASTA

Preparation time: 15 minutes
Total cooking time: 30 minutes
Serves 4

100 g (3½ oz) butter
500 g (1 lb) veal schnitzel, cut into
　　bite-sized pieces
300 g (10 oz) Swiss brown
　　mushrooms, sliced
3 cloves garlic, crushed
¾ cup (185 ml/6 fl oz) dry white wine
½ cup (125 ml/4 fl oz) chicken stock
200 ml (6½ fl oz) thick cream
1–2 tablespoons lemon juice
400 g (13 oz) pappardelle

**1** Melt half the butter in a large frying pan over medium heat. Add the veal in batches and cook for 2–3 minutes, or until golden brown. Remove the veal from the pan and keep warm.

**2** Add the remaining butter to the same pan and heat until foaming. Add the mushrooms and garlic and cook, stirring, over low heat for 5 minutes. Pour in the wine and stock, scraping the bottom of the pan with a wooden spoon, and simmer, covered, for 10 minutes.

**3** Remove the lid, add the cream and simmer for 5 minutes, or until the sauce thickens. Stir in the lemon juice, veal and any juices until warmed through. Season to taste. Meanwhile, cook the pasta in a large pan of rapidly boiling salted water until *al dente*. Drain well, toss the sauce through the pasta and serve immediately.

NUTRITION PER SERVE
Protein 45 g; Fat 41 g; Carbohydrate 74 g;
Dietary Fibre 5 g; Cholesterol 236 mg;
3660 kJ (875 cal)

Cook the veal in the butter in batches until it is golden brown.

Add the cream to the sauce and then simmer uncovered to allow it to thicken.

## FARFALLE WITH SPINACH AND BACON

Preparation time: 10 minutes
Total cooking time: 15 minutes
Serves 4

400 g (13 oz) farfalle
2 tablespoons extra virgin olive oil
250 g (8 oz) bacon, chopped
1 red onion, finely chopped
250 g (8 oz) baby spinach leaves
1–2 tablespoons sweet chilli sauce
1/4 cup (30 g/1 oz) crumbled feta
   cheese

**1** Cook the pasta in a large pan of rapidly boiling salted water until *al dente*. Drain and return to the pan to keep warm.
**2** Meanwhile, heat the oil in a frying pan, add the bacon and cook over medium heat for 3 minutes, or until golden. Add the onion and cook for a further 4 minutes, or until softened. Toss the spinach leaves through the onion and bacon mixture for 30 seconds, or until just wilted.
**3** Add the bacon and spinach mixture to the drained pasta, then stir in the sweet chilli sauce. Season to taste with salt and cracked black pepper and toss well. Spoon into warm pasta bowls and scatter with the crumbled feta. Serve immediately.

NUTRITION PER SERVE
Protein 28 g; Fat 19 g; Carbohydrate 73 g;
Dietary Fibre 7 g; Cholesterol 42 mg;
2415 kJ (575 cal)

Cook the bacon over medium heat for 3 minutes or until golden.

Add the bacon and spinach to the drained pasta and stir in the sweet chilli sauce.

# CREAMY RIGATONI WITH CHICKEN AND SUN-DRIED TOMATO SAUCE

Preparation time: 5 minutes
Total cooking time: 20 minutes
Serves 4–6

500 g (1 lb) rigatoni
1 tablespoon olive oil
4 chicken breast fillets, thinly sliced
4 ripe tomatoes, diced
150 g (5 oz) sun-dried tomatoes in oil, thinly sliced
2 tablespoons sun-dried tomato paste (see NOTE)
handful of small fresh basil leaves
300 ml (10 fl oz) cream
200 ml (6½ fl oz) chicken stock

**1** Cook the pasta in a large pan of rapidly boiling salted water until *al dente*. Drain and return to the pan to keep warm.
**2** Meanwhile, heat the oil in a deep frying pan and cook the chicken over high heat for 4 minutes each side, or until browned and cooked through. Remove from the pan and keep warm.
**3** Return the pan to the heat and add the tomato, sun-dried tomato, sun-dried tomato paste and half the basil leaves. Cook over medium heat for 5 minutes, or until the tomato starts to soften. Stir in the cream and chicken stock and bring to the boil, stirring constantly.
**4** Reduce the heat and return the chicken to the pan. Add the rigatoni and season with pepper. Heat gently until the chicken and pasta are warmed through. Top with the remaining basil leaves and serve immediately with crusty bread.

NUTRITION PER SERVE (6)
Protein 45 g; Fat 50 g; Carbohydrate 90 g; Dietary Fibre 8 g; Cholesterol 195 mg; 4227 kJ (1010 cal)

NOTE: Sun-dried tomato paste is available in good supermarkets. Or, you can make your own by processing whole sun-dried tomatoes in oil with a little of their oil until a smooth paste is formed.

Drain the cooked rigatoni and then return to the pan to keep warm.

Cook the chicken over high heat until browned and cooked through.

Cook the tomato, sun-dried tomato, sun-dried tomato paste and half the basil.

Return the chicken to the pan and toss through the rigatoni.

## SALMON AND RICOTTA-STUFFED CONCHIGLIONE

Preparation time: 15 minutes
Total cooking time: 50 minutes
Serves 4

200 g (6½ oz) conchiglione (large pasta shells)
425 g (14 oz) can red salmon, drained, bones removed, flaked
500 g (1 lb) ricotta
1 tablespoon chopped fresh flat-leaf parsley
3 tablespoons chopped fresh chives
1½ celery stalks, finely chopped
¾ cup (90 g/3 oz) grated Cheddar
¾ cup (185 ml/6 fl oz) cream
¼ cup (30 g/1 oz) grated Parmesan

**1** Preheat the oven to moderate 180°C (350°F/Gas 4). Cook the pasta in a large pan of rapidly boiling salted water until *al dente*. Drain and return to the pan to keep warm.
**2** Combine the salmon, ricotta, parsley, chives, celery and Cheddar in a bowl and season to taste with salt and cracked black pepper.

**3** Place 2 teaspoons of filling in each shell and arrange in a single layer in a 3-litre ovenproof dish. Pour on the cream and sprinkle with Parmesan. Cover with foil and bake for 20 minutes, then remove the foil and return to the oven for 15 minutes, or until golden brown. Serve with the sauce spooned over the shells.

NUTRITION PER SERVE
Protein 31 g; Fat 36 g; Carbohydrate 38 g; Dietary Fibre 3 g; Cholesterol 135 mg; 2470 kJ (590 cal)

Cook the large pasta shells until they are tender, then drain.

Mix together the salmon, ricotta, parsley, chives, celery and Cheddar.

Arrange the shells in a single layer in the dish, then top with the cream and Parmesan.

# VEGETARIAN LASAGNE

Preparation time: 1 hour
Total cooking time: 1 hour 30 minutes
Serves 8

500 g (1 lb) fresh spinach lasagne
    sheets
1/2 cup (30 g/1 oz) fresh basil leaves,
    coarsely chopped
2 tablespoons fresh breadcrumbs
3 tablespoons pine nuts
2 teaspoons paprika
1 tablespoon grated Parmesan

RICOTTA FILLING
750 g (1 1/2 lb) ricotta
1/2 cup (50 g/1 3/4 oz) grated
    Parmesan
pinch of nutmeg

TOMATO SAUCE
1 tablespoon olive oil
2 onions, chopped
2 cloves garlic, crushed
800 g (1 lb 10 oz) can crushed
    tomatoes
1 tablespoon tomato paste

BECHAMEL SAUCE
60 g (2 oz) butter
1/2 cup (60 g/2 oz) plain flour
2 cups (500 ml/16 fl oz) milk
2 eggs, lightly beaten
1/3 cup (30 g/1 oz) grated Parmesan

**1** Lightly grease a 25 x 32 cm (10 x 13 inch) baking dish. Cut the pasta sheets into large pieces and cook, a couple at a time, in boiling water for 3 minutes. Drain and spread on damp tea towels until needed.
**2** To make the ricotta filling, put the ricotta and Parmesan cheeses and nutmeg in a bowl and mix together well. Season with black pepper and set aside.
**3** To make the tomato sauce, heat the oil in a frying pan, add the onion and cook for about 10 minutes, stirring occasionally, until very soft. Add the garlic and cook for 1 more minute. Add the tomato and tomato paste and stir until well combined. Stir until the mixture comes to the boil. Reduce the heat and simmer uncovered for 15 minutes, or until thickened, stirring occasionally.
**4** To make the Béchamel sauce, heat the butter in a small pan. When starting to foam, add the flour and stir for 3 minutes, or until just coloured. Remove from the heat; add the milk gradually, stirring after each addition, then return to the heat and stir until the sauce boils and thickens. Remove from the heat and stir in the eggs. Return to moderate heat and stir until almost boiling, but do not boil. Add the cheese and season to taste. Put plastic wrap onto the surface to prevent a skin forming. Preheat the oven to 200°C (400°F/Gas 6).
**5** Put a layer of lasagne sheets in the dish. Spread with a third of the ricotta filling, sprinkle with basil, then top with a third of the tomato sauce. Repeat the layers, finishing with pasta.
**6** Pour over the Béchamel sauce, spread until smooth, then sprinkle with the combined breadcrumbs, pine nuts, paprika and Parmesan. Bake for 45 minutes, or until browned. Leave to stand for 10 minutes before serving.

NUTRITION PER SERVE
Protein 22 g; Fat 30 g; Carbohydrate 16 g;
Dietary Fibre 14 g; Cholesterol 130 mg;
1750 kJ (416 cal)

Cook the lasagne in a large pan of boiling water, a couple of sheets at a time.

Simmer the tomato sauce, uncovered, for 15 minutes until it has thickened.

Stir the Béchamel sauce over the heat until it boils and thickens.

Placing plastic wrap onto the surface of the sauce will stop a skin forming.

Use the back of a spoon to spread a layer of tomato sauce over the ricotta filling.

Sprinkle the pine nut and breadcrumb mixture over the Béchamel sauce.

# BAKED SEAFOOD PASTA

Preparation time: 15 minutes
Total cooking time: 45 minutes
Serves 4–6

250 g (8 oz) lasagne sheets
500 g (1 lb) boneless fish fillets
125 g (4 oz) scallops, cleaned
500 g (1 lb) raw prawns, peeled and
  deveined
125 g (4 oz) butter
1 leek, sliced
2/3 cup (90 g/3 oz) plain flour
2 cups (500 ml/16 fl oz) milk
2 cups (500 ml/16 fl oz) dry white wine
1 cup (125 g/4 oz) grated Cheddar
1/2 cup (125 ml/4 fl oz) cream
1/2 cup (60 g/2 oz) grated Parmesan
2 tablespoons chopped fresh parsley

**1** Preheat the oven to moderate 180°C
(350°F/Gas 4). Line a greased shallow
24 x 30 cm (10 x 12 inch) ovenproof
dish with lasagne sheets, breaking
them to fill any gaps. Chop the fish
and scallops into even-sized pieces.
Chop the prawns.
**2** Melt the butter in a large pan and
cook the leek, stirring, for 1 minute.
Add the flour and cook, stirring, for
1 minute. Remove from the heat and
slowly stir in the milk and wine until
smooth. Return to medium heat and
stir constantly until the sauce boils and
thickens. Reduce the heat and simmer
for 3 minutes. Stir in the cheese and
seafood, season and simmer for
1 minute.
**3** Spoon half the seafood sauce over
the lasagne sheets. Top with another
layer of lasagne sheets. Continue
layering, finishing with lasagne sheets.
**4** Pour the cream over the top.
Sprinkle with the combined Parmesan
and parsley and bake for 30 minutes
or until bubbling and golden.

NUTRITION PER SERVE (6)
Protein 57 g; Fat 28 g; Carbohydrate 45 g;
Dietary Fibre 3 g; Cholesterol 264 mg;
3000 kJ (720 cal)

Cut the fish and scallops into bite-sized pieces
and chop the prawns.

Slowly stir in the wine and milk and stir until the
sauce is smooth.

Build up the layers of seafood sauce and lasagne
sheets in the dish.

Mix together the Parmesan and parsley and
sprinkle over the top.

# SPINACH AND RICOTTA CANNELLONI

Preparation time: 45 minutes
Total cooking time: 1 hour
Serves 4

### FILLING
30 g (1 oz) butter
1 small onion, finely chopped
2 cloves garlic, crushed
3 bunches English spinach, trimmed and finely shredded
300 g (10 oz) ricotta cheese
1 tablespoon fresh oregano

### SAUCE
1 tablespoon olive oil
1 small onion, finely chopped
2 cloves garlic, crushed
440 g (14 oz) can peeled whole tomatoes
1/2 cup (125 ml/4 fl oz) tomato pasta sauce
1 teaspoon dried oregano
2 teaspoons Dijon mustard
1 tablespoon balsamic vinegar
1 teaspoon sugar

375 g (12 oz) packet fresh lasagne
1/2 cup (75 g/2 1/2 oz) grated mozzarella
1/2 cup (50 g/1 3/4 oz) finely grated Parmesan

**1** Preheat the oven to moderate 180°C (350°F/Gas 4). Cut the pasta sheets into twelve 12 cm squares. Bring a pan of salted water to the boil, blanch the lasagne in batches for 1–2 minutes, then drain flat on a damp tea towel.
**2** Melt the butter in a pan and cook the onion and garlic for 3–5 minutes, or until the onion softens. Add the spinach and cook for 5 minutes, or until wilted and the moisture has evaporated. Cool then mix with the ricotta and oregano in a food processor until smooth. Season.
**3** To make the sauce, heat the oil in a pan, add the onion and garlic and cook over low heat for 8–10 minutes. Add the rest of the sauce ingredients. Bring to the boil, then reduce the heat and simmer for 10–15 minutes, or until the sauce thickens.
**4** Lightly grease a 2 litre (64 fl oz) casserole. Spread a third of the sauce over the base. Spoon 1 1/2 tablespoons of spinach mixture onto one side of each lasagne square, leaving a small border. Roll up the pasta to cover the filling and place in the dish seam-side-down. Repeat with all the sheets. Spoon in the remaining sauce and sprinkle with the cheeses. Bake for 30–35 minutes, or until bubbling. Leave for 5 minutes before serving.

NUTRITION PER SERVE
Protein 25 g; Fat 27 g; Carbohydrate 35 g; Dietary Fibre 5 g; Cholesterol 70 mg; 1970 kJ (470 cal)

Blanch the lasagne sheets in batches in salted boiling water.

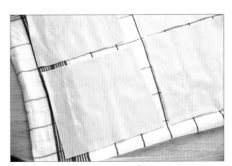
Lay the lasagne squares out flat on a clean damp tea towel to drain.

Spoon the spinach mixture onto one side of the pasta square and then roll up into a tube.

# risottos

## LEEK AND PROSCIUTTO RISOTTO WITH PARSLEY PISTOU

Preparation time: 10 minutes
Total cooking time: 45 minutes
Serves 2

PARSLEY PISTOU
¼ cup (60 ml/2 fl oz) extra virgin olive
   oil
1 clove garlic, crushed
2 tablespoons chopped fresh
   flat-leaf parsley

100 g (3½ oz) prosciutto
3 cups (750 ml/24 fl oz) chicken stock
60 g (2 oz) butter
2 leeks, halved lengthways and sliced
1 celery stick, sliced thinly
2 cups (440 g/14 oz) arborio rice
½ cup (125 ml/4 fl oz) dry white wine
2 teaspoons fresh thyme

**1** To make the pistou, combine the oil, garlic, parsley and ½ teaspoon cracked pepper in a blender or mortar and pestle and blend until combined.
**2** Place the prosciutto on an oven tray lined with foil and cook under a hot grill for 3 minutes, or until crisp—be careful not to burn it. Cool, then break into small pieces.
**3** Put the stock and 3 cups (750 ml/ 24 fl oz) water in a pan, bring to the boil, then reduce to simmering.
**4** Heat the butter over medium heat in a large heavy-based pan. When foaming, add the leek and cook, stirring occasionally, for 7 minutes, or until soft. Add the celery and rice and stir for 1 minute, or until the rice is coated in the butter. Add the wine, allow it to boil until almost dry, then add ½ cup (125 ml/4 fl oz) of the hot

stock and stir over low heat with a wooden spoon until all the liquid is absorbed. Continue adding the stock a ladleful at a time, stirring continuously until it is completely absorbed before the next addition. The risotto will be ready after 20–25 minutes when the rice grains are swollen and the mixture appears creamy. You may not need to use all the stock. The rice should be just

tender, when bitten, but not chalky. Stir in the prosciutto and thyme, and season to taste with salt. Spoon into serving bowls and swirl through some of the pistou. Serve immediately.

NUTRITION PER SERVE
Protein 15 g; Fat 55 g; Carbohydrate 175 g;
Dietary Fibre 7 g; Cholesterol 75 mg;
5465 kJ (1305 Cal)

Stir in the celery and rice until the rice is coated in butter.

Add the wine and allow the mixture to boil until almost dry.

Pour in a ladleful of stock and stir until completely absorbed.

# MUSHROOM RISOTTO

Preparation time: 15 minutes
Total cooking time: 40 minutes
Serves 4

1.5 litres vegetable stock
2 cups (500 ml/16 fl oz) white wine
2 tablespoons olive oil
60 g (2 oz) butter
2 leeks, thinly sliced
1 kg (2 lb) flat mushrooms, sliced
500 g (1 lb) arborio rice
3/4 cup (75 g/2½ oz) grated Parmesan, plus Parmesan shavings, to serve

3 tablespoons chopped fresh flat-leaf parsley
balsamic vinegar and fresh flat-leaf parsley, to serve

**1** Place the stock and wine in a large saucepan and keep at simmering point on the stove top.
**2** Heat the oil and butter in a large saucepan. Add the leek and cook over medium heat for 5 minutes, or until soft and golden. Add the mushrooms to the pan and cook for 5 minutes, or until tender. Add the rice and stir for 1 minute, or until translucent.
**3** Add ½ cup (125 ml/4 fl oz) hot stock, stirring constantly over medium heat until the liquid is absorbed. Continue adding the stock, a little at a time, stirring constantly for 20–25 minutes, or until all the rice is tender and creamy (you may not need all the stock, or you may need to add a little water if you run out).
**4** Stir in the Parmesan and chopped parsley and heat for 1 minute, or until all the cheese has melted. Serve drizzled with balsamic vinegar and topped with Parmesan shavings.

NUTRITION PER SERVE
Protein 26 g; Fat 30 g; Carbohydrate 105 g; Dietary Fibre 11 g; Cholesterol 56 mg; 3299 kJ (788 Cal)

Cook the leek and mushrooms in a large saucepan until tender.

Stir the rice constantly until most of the liquid has been absorbed.

Once the rice is tender, stir the grated Parmesan and parsley into the risotto.

## PUMPKIN AND BROAD BEAN RISOTTO

Preparation time: 35 minutes
Total cooking time: 50 minutes
Serves 4

350 g (11 oz) pumpkin
cooking oil spray
1 tablespoon olive oil
1 large onion, finely chopped
2 cloves garlic, finely chopped
3 cups (750 ml/24 fl oz) vegetable
   stock
1 cup (220 g/7 oz) arborio rice
200 g (6 1/2 oz) Swiss brown
   mushrooms, halved

2 cups (310 g/10 oz) frozen broad
   beans, defrosted, peeled
4 tablespoons grated Parmesan

**1** Preheat the oven to moderately hot 200°C (400°F/Gas 6). Cut the pumpkin into small chunks, place on a baking tray and spray lightly with oil. Bake, turning occasionally, for 20 minutes, or until tender. Set aside, covered.
**2** Meanwhile, heat the oil in a large heavy-based pan, add the onion and garlic, cover and cook for 10 minutes over low heat. Put the stock in a different pan and keep at simmering point on the stove top.
**3** Add the rice to the onion and stir for 2 minutes. Gradually stir in 1/2 cup

(125 ml/4 fl oz) of the hot stock, until absorbed. Stir in another 1/2 cup (125 ml/4 fl oz) of hot stock until absorbed. Add the mushrooms and continue adding the remaining stock, a little at a time, until it is all absorbed and the rice is just tender (this will take about 25 minutes).
**4** Stir in the cooked pumpkin and the broad beans. Sprinkle with the grated Parmesan.

NUTRITION PER SERVE
Protein 20 g; Fat 12 g; Carbohydrate 60 g; Dietary Fibre 10 g; Cholesterol 20 mg; 1775 kJ (425 Cal)

Put the chunks of pumpkin on a baking tray and spray with oil.

Add the stock to the rice, a little at a time, and stir until absorbed.

Add the mushrooms, then continue stirring in the stock until absorbed.

# FENNEL RISOTTO BALLS WITH CHEESY FILLING

Preparation time: 30 minutes +
 30 minutes refrigeration
Total cooking time: 50 minutes
Serves 4–6

1.5 litres vegetable stock
1 tablespoon oil
30 g (1 oz) butter
2 cloves garlic, crushed
1 onion, finely chopped
2 fennel bulbs, finely sliced
1 tablespoon balsamic vinegar
1/2 cup (125 ml/4 fl oz) white wine
3 cups (660 g/1 lb 5 oz) arborio rice
1/2 cup (50 g/1 3/4 oz) grated
 Parmesan
1/2 cup (25 g/3/4 oz) snipped fresh
 chives
1 egg, lightly beaten
150 g (5 oz) sun-dried tomatoes,
 chopped
100 g (3 1/2 oz) mozzarella, diced
1/2 cup (90 g/3 oz) frozen peas,
 thawed
flour, for dusting
3 eggs, lightly beaten, extra
2 cups (200 g/6 1/2 oz) dry
 breadcrumbs
oil, for deep-frying

**1** Heat the stock in a saucepan and keep at simmering point.
**2** Heat the oil and butter in a large saucepan and cook the garlic and onion for 3 minutes, or until soft. Add the fennel and cook for 10 minutes, or until it starts to caramelise. Add the vinegar and wine, increase the heat and boil until the liquid evaporates. Add the rice and stir for 1 minute, or until translucent.
**3** Add 1/2 cup (125 ml/4 fl oz) hot stock, stirring constantly over medium heat until the liquid is absorbed. Continue adding stock, stirring, for 20–25 minutes, or until the rice is tender and creamy. Stir in the Parmesan, chives, egg and tomato. Place in a bowl, cover and cool.
**4** Place the mozzarella and peas in a bowl and mash together. Season.
**5** With wet hands, shape the risotto into 14 even balls. Flatten each ball out, slightly indenting the centre. Place

a heaped teaspoon of the pea mash into the indentation, then re-form to make a ball. Roll each ball in seasoned flour, then dip in the extra egg and roll in breadcrumbs. Place on a foil-covered tray and chill for 30 minutes.
**6** Fill a deep heavy-based saucepan one-third full of oil and heat to 180°C (350°F), or until a cube of bread browns in 15 seconds. Cook the risotto balls in batches for 5 minutes, or until

golden and crisp and the cheese has melted inside. Drain on crumpled paper towels and season with salt. If the cheese has not melted, cook the balls on a tray in a moderate 180°C (350°F/ Gas 4) oven for 5 minutes.

NUTRITION PER SERVE (6)
Protein 11 g; Fat 9.5 g; Carbohydrate 48 g;
Dietary Fibre 2.5 g; Cholesterol 65 mg;
1377 kJ (329 Cal)

Stir the Parmesan, chives, egg and sun-dried tomato into the risotto.

Place a heaped teaspoon of the cheesy pea mixture into the middle of each ball.

## ASPARAGUS AND PISTACHIO RISOTTO

Preparation time: 10 minutes
Total cooking time: 30 minutes
Serves 4–6

1 litre vegetable stock
1 cup (250 ml/8 fl oz) white wine
1/3 cup (80 ml/2 3/4 fl oz) extra virgin
   olive oil
1 red onion, finely chopped
2 cups (440 g/14 oz) arborio rice
310 g (10 oz) asparagus spears,
   trimmed and cut into short lengths
1/2 cup (125 ml/4 fl oz) cream

1 cup (100 g/3 1/2 oz) grated
   Parmesan
1/2 cup (75 g/2 1/2 oz) shelled pistachio
   nuts, toasted and roughly chopped

**1** Heat the stock and wine in a large saucepan and keep at simmering point on the stove top.
**2** Heat the oil in another large saucepan. Add the onion and cook over medium heat for 3 minutes, or until soft. Add the rice and stir for 1 minute, or until translucent.
**3** Add 1/2 cup (125 ml/4 fl oz) hot stock, stirring constantly until the liquid is absorbed. Continue adding more stock, a little at a time, stirring

constantly for 20–25 minutes, or until the rice is tender and creamy (you may not need to add all the stock, or you may not have quite enough and will need to add a little water as well—every risotto is different). Add the asparagus during the last 5 minutes of cooking.
**4** Remove from the heat and leave for 2 minutes, then stir in the cream and Parmesan and season well. Serve sprinkled with pistachios.

NUTRITION PER SERVE (6)
Protein 15 g; Fat 30 g; Carbohydrate 60 g;
Dietary Fibre 3.5 g; Cholesterol 45 mg;
2425 kJ (580 Cal)

Add the rice to the saucepan and stir until the grains are translucent.

Add the stock a little at a time, stirring until it is completely absorbed.

Leave the risotto to stand for 2 minutes, then stir in the cream and Parmesan.

# BAKED CHICKEN AND LEEK RISOTTO

Preparation time: 10 minutes
Total cooking time: 40 minutes
Serves 6
Fat per serve: 15 g

1 tablespoon oil
1 leek, thinly sliced
2 chicken breast fillets, cubed
2 cups (440 g/14 oz) arborio rice
1/4 cup (60 ml/2 fl oz) white wine
5 cups (1.25) litres chicken stock
1/3 cup (30 g/1 oz) grated Parmesan
2 tablespoons fresh thyme leaves
fresh thyme leaves and Parmesan, for
      serving

**1** Preheat the oven to slow 150°C (300°F/Gas 2) and place a 5 litre ovenproof dish with a lid in the oven to warm. Heat the oil in a saucepan over medium heat, add the leek and cook for 2 minutes, or until soft.
**2** Add the chicken and cook, stirring, for 2–3 minutes, or until it colours. Add the rice and stir so that it is well coated. Cook for 1 minute.
**3** Add the wine and stock and bring to the boil. Pour the mixture into the warm ovenproof dish and cover. Place in the oven and cook for 30 minutes, stirring halfway through. Remove from the oven and stir through the Parmesan and thyme leaves. Season to taste. Sprinkle with extra thyme leaves and a little Parmesan and serve.

NUTRITION PER SERVE
Protein 28 g; Fat 15 g; Carbohydrate 60 g;
Dietary Fibre 3 g; Cholesterol 75 mg;
2014 kJ (480 cal)

Cook the leek for a couple of minutes over medium heat until it is soft.

Add the arborio rice to the pan and stir until it is well coated.

Cook the risotto in the oven for 30 minutes, then remove and stir in the Parmesan and thyme.

# SEAFOOD AND HERB RISOTTO

Preparation time: 40 minutes
Total cooking time: 50 minutes
Serves 4

150 g (5 oz) white boneless fish fillet
such as sea perch
8 black mussels (200 g/6 1/2 oz)
8 raw prawns (250 g/8 oz)
1.75 litres chicken stock
cooking oil spray
2 onions, finely chopped
2 cloves garlic, finely chopped
1 celery stick, finely chopped
2 cups (440 g/14 oz) arborio rice
(see NOTE)
2 tablespoons chopped fresh parsley
1 tablespoon chopped fresh oregano
1 tablespoon chopped fresh thyme
leaves
2 tablespoons grated Parmesan

**1** Cut the fish fillet into small cubes. Scrub the mussels well and remove the beards. Discard any mussels that are broken or open and do not close when tapped. Peel and devein the prawns, leaving the tails intact. Put the seafood in a bowl and refrigerate until required.
**2** Put the stock in a saucepan and bring to the boil, then reduce the heat until just gently simmering.
**3** Lightly spray a large saucepan with cooking oil and heat over medium heat. Add the onion, garlic and celery and cook for 2–3 minutes. Add 2 tablespoons water, cover and cook for 5 minutes, or until the vegetables have begun to soften. Add the arborio rice and 2 tablespoons water and stir over medium heat for 3–4 minutes, or until the rice grains are well coated.

**4** Gradually add 1/2 cup (125 ml/ 4 fl oz) of the hot stock to the rice mixture, stirring constantly over low heat with a wooden spoon, until all the stock has been absorbed. Repeat the process, adding 1/2 cup (125 ml/4 fl oz) of liquid each time until all but a small amount of stock is left and the rice is just tender.
**5** Meanwhile, bring a small amount of water to the boil in a saucepan. Add the mussels, cover and cook for about 3 minutes, shaking the pan occasionally, until the mussels have opened. Drain the mussels and discard any that have not opened in the cooking time.
**6** Add the fish and prawns and the remaining hot stock to the rice. Stir well and continue to cook for about 5–10 minutes, or until the seafood is just cooked and the rice is tender and creamy. Remove from the heat, add the cooked mussels, cover and set aside for 5 minutes. Stir the herbs and Parmesan through the risotto, then season well. Serve immediately.

NUTRITION PER SERVE
Protein 40 g; Fat 5 g; Carbohydrate 90 g;
Dietary Fibre 4 g; Cholesterol 175 mg;
2395 kJ (570 Cal)

NOTE: Arborio has a fatter and shorter grain than other short-grain rice. The chief ingredient of risotto, arborio has a high starch content which gives the dish its creamy texture. This is the reason you can't successfully use another type of rice.

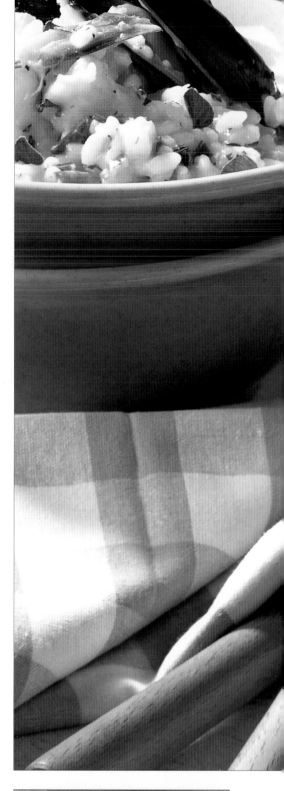

Scrub the mussels thoroughly and pull off the beards. Discard any open mussels.

Add the arborio rice to the pan and stir over the heat until the rice is well coated.

Stir in the stock a little at a time, not adding any more until the last portion has been absorbed.

Risotto is ready when the rice has absorbed all the hot stock.

Put the mussels in a pan of boiling water, cover and cook for 3 minutes to open them.

Stir the chopped herbs and grated Parmesan through the risotto.

## RISOTTO WITH SCALLOPS AND MINTED PEAS

Preparation time: 15 minutes
Total cooking time: 35 minutes
Serves 4–6

1 litre chicken, fish or vegetable stock
2¾ cups (360 g/12 oz) fresh or frozen baby peas
2 tablespoons light sour cream
2 tablespoons finely shredded fresh mint
1 tablespoon olive oil
1 small onion, finely chopped
2 cloves garlic, finely chopped
150 g (5 oz) arborio rice
16 large scallops (without roe)
1 tablespoon grated fresh Parmesan
4 fresh mint leaves, to garnish
lemon wedges, to serve

**1** Bring the stock to the boil and add the peas. Simmer for 1–2 minutes, or until the peas are tender, then remove with a slotted spoon and keep the stock at a low simmer. Blend 1¾ cups (230 g/7½ oz) of the peas with the sour cream in a food processor until smooth. Season, then stir in 1 tablespoon of the mint.
**2** Place the oil in a large shallow saucepan and cook the onion over low heat for 4–5 minutes, or until just soft. Add the garlic and cook for 30 seconds. Stir in the rice to coat. Increase the heat to medium.
**3** Add 1 cup (250 ml/8 fl oz) stock to the rice mixture and cook, stirring constantly, until all the liquid has evaporated. Add the stock, ½ cup (125 ml/4 fl oz) at a time until the rice is cooked and the mixture is creamy.

This will take about 20 minutes.
**4** Lightly season the scallops. Heat a chargrill pan or hotplate, add the scallops and sear on both sides until cooked to your liking.
**5** Fold the pea purée through the risotto with the whole peas and Parmesan. Divide the risotto among serving bowls and place the scallops on top. Sprinkle with the remaining mint, garnish with a fresh mint leaf and serve with a wedge of lemon.

NUTRITION PER SERVE (6)
Protein 12.5 g; Fat 6 g; Carbohydrate 27.5 g; Dietary Fibre 4.5 g; Cholesterol 17 mg; 895 kJ (215 Cal)

Process the peas and sour cream in a food processor until smooth.

Fold the pea purée, reserved whole peas and Parmesan through the risotto.

## CARROT AND PUMPKIN RISOTTO

Preparation time: 15 minutes
Total cooking time: 35 minutes
Serves 4

90 g (3 oz) butter
1 onion, finely chopped
250 g (8 oz) pumpkin, diced
2 carrots, diced
2 litres vegetable stock
2 cups (440 g/14 oz) arborio rice
90 g (3 oz) Romano cheese, grated
   (see NOTE)
1/4 teaspoon nutmeg

**1** Heat 60 g (2 oz) of the butter in a large, heavy-based pan. Add the onion and fry for 1–2 minutes, or until soft. Add the pumpkin and carrot and cook for 6–8 minutes, or until tender. Mash slightly with a potato masher. In a separate saucepan keep the stock at simmering point.

**2** Add the rice to the vegetables and cook for 1 minute, stirring constantly until the grains are translucent. Ladle in 1/2 cup (125 ml/4 fl oz) hot stock and stir well. Reduce the heat and add the stock little by little, stirring constantly for 20–25 minutes, or until the rice is tender and creamy. (You may not need to add all the stock, or you may run out and need to use a little water. Every risotto is different.)

**3** Remove from the heat, add the remaining butter, cheese, nutmeg and pepper and fork through. Cover and leave for 5 minutes before serving.

NUTRITION PER SERVE
Protein 27 g; Fat 34 g; Carbohydrate 95 g; Dietary Fibre 5 g; Cholesterol 100 mg; 3318 kJ (793 Cal)

NOTE: Romano is a hard, Italian grating cheese similar to Parmesan. Parmesan is a good substitute.

Heat the butter in a large pan and fry the onion until soft.

Cook the pumpkin and carrot until tender, then mash a little.

The secret to good risotto is to add the stock a little at a time and stir constantly.

# chargrills, barbecues
# & pan-fries

## VEAL STEAKS WITH CAPER BUTTER

Preparation time: 10 minutes
Total cooking time: 6 minutes
Serves 4

50 g (1³/₄ oz) butter, softened
2 tablespoons dry white wine
2 tablespoons capers, finely chopped
2 teaspoons finely grated lemon rind
8 small veal steaks, about 500 g (1 lb)

**1** Mix together the butter, white wine, capers, lemon rind and some salt and black pepper with a wooden spoon. Cover and refrigerate until required.
**2** Cook the veal steaks on a hot, lightly oiled barbecue flatplate or grill for 2–3 minutes on each side. Remove, place on warm plates and top with the caper butter. Serve immediately.

NUTRITION PER SERVE
Protein 30 g; Fat 15 g; Carbohydrate 0 g;
Dietary Fibre 0 g; Cholesterol 135 mg;
990 kJ (235 cal)

Use a sharp knife to finely chop the capers so that they mix smoothly with the butter.

Mix the butter, white wine, capers, lemon rind and salt and pepper.

Cook the veal for 2–3 minutes on each side on a hot barbecue flatplate.

## CHICKEN WITH SALSA VERDE

Preparation time: 10 minutes
Total cooking time: 10 minutes
Serves 6

SALSA VERDE
1 clove garlic
2 cups (60 g/2 oz) firmly packed fresh
 flat-leaf parsley
1/3 cup (80 ml/2³/4 fl oz) extra virgin
 olive oil

3 tablespoons chopped fresh dill
1¹/2 tablespoons Dijon mustard
1 tablespoon sherry vinegar
1 tablespoon baby capers, drained

6 large chicken breast fillets

**1** Place all the ingredients for the salsa verde in a food processor or blender and process until almost smooth.
**2** Cook the chicken fillets on a very hot, lightly oiled barbecue grill or flatplate for 4–5 minutes each side, or until cooked through.

**3** Cut each chicken fillet into three on the diagonal and arrange on serving plates. Top with a spoonful of salsa verde and season to taste.

NUTRITION PER SERVE
Protein 50 g; Fat 18 g; Carbohydrate 0 g;
Dietary Fibre 0.5 g; Cholesterol 110 mg;
1510 kJ (360 cal)

STORAGE: The salsa verde can be kept for a day in the fridge.

Put all the salsa verde ingredients in the food processor and process until almost smooth.

Cook the chicken on a very hot barbecue until it is cooked through.

To serve, slice each fillet into three on the diagonal and top with salsa verde.

# CHARGRILLED VEGETABLES

Preparation time: 15 minutes +
  40 minutes standing
Total cooking time: 1 hour
Serves 6

2 eggplants
900 g (1¾ lb) orange sweet potato
4 zucchini
2 red capsicums
600 g (1¼ lb) button mushrooms
⅓ cup (80 ml/2¾ fl oz) olive oil

BASIL DRESSING
½ cup (125 ml/4 fl oz) olive oil
2 cloves garlic, crushed
2 tablespoons balsamic vinegar
½ teaspoon sugar
⅓ cup (20 g/¾ oz) fresh basil leaves

**1** Cut the eggplant into 1 cm (½ inch) thick slices. Place on a wire rack and sprinkle liberally with salt. Leave for 30 minutes, then rinse under cold water and pat dry with paper towels.
**2** Cut the sweet potato into 5 mm (¼ inch) slices and the zucchini into 1 cm (½ inch) slices lengthways. Quarter the capsicums, remove the seeds and membranes and chargrill, skin-side-down, until the skin blackens and blisters. (Alternatively, cook the capsicums, skin-side-up, under a preheated grill to blister the skins.) Place in a plastic bag and leave to cool. Peel away the skin.
**3** Brush the eggplant, sweet potato, zucchini and mushrooms with oil. Chargrill or barbecue in batches until lightly browned and cooked through.
**4** To make the basil dressing, put the oil, garlic, vinegar, sugar and basil in a food processor or blender and process until smooth.
**5** Combine the chargrilled vegetables with the basil dressing and mix well. Allow to cool, then cover and refrigerate until ready to use. Return to room temperature before serving.

NUTRITION PER SERVE
Protein 9 g; Fat 20 g; Carbohydrate 28 g; Dietary Fibre 9 g; Cholesterol 0 mg; 1495 kJ (355 Cal)

Put the slices of eggplant on a wire rack and sprinkle with salt.

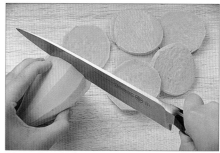

Use a sharp knife to cut the sweet potato into slices.

Once cooled, gently peel the blackened skin off the capsicums.

Brush the vegetables with oil and chargrill or barbecue until lightly browned.

# LAMB CUTLETS WITH ROSEMARY MARINADE

Preparation time: 15 minutes +
　20 minutes marinating
Total cooking time: 10 minutes
Serves 4

12 lamb cutlets
3 tablespoons olive oil
2 tablespoons chopped fresh
　rosemary
1¹/₂ teaspoons cracked black pepper
1 bunch fresh rosemary, extra

**1** Trim the cutlets of excess fat and sinew. Place in a shallow, non-metallic dish and brush with oil.
**2** Scatter half the chopped rosemary and pepper on the meat and set aside for 20 minutes. Turn the meat over and brush with the remaining oil. Scatter with the remaining rosemary and pepper. Tie the extra bunch of rosemary to the handle of a wooden spoon.
**3** Cook the cutlets on a hot, lightly oiled barbecue grill or flatplate for 2–3 minutes on each side. As the cutlets cook, bat frequently with the rosemary spoon. This will release flavoursome oils into the cutlets. When the cutlets are almost done, remove the rosemary from the spoon and drop it on the fire, where it will flare up briefly and infuse rosemary smoke into the cutlets. Serve with barbecued lemon slices.

NUTRITION PER SERVE
Protein 23 g; Fat 22 g; Carbohydrate 0 g;
Dietary Fibre 0 g; Cholesterol 71 mg;
1195 kJ (285 cal)

Trim the lamb cutlets of excess fat and sinew and then place in a shallow dish.

Scatter half the chopped rosemary and pepper over the meat.

As the lamb is cooking, bat it frequently with the rosemary spoon to add flavour.

# CHICKEN WITH OLIVES AND SUN-DRIED TOMATOES

Preparation time: 20 minutes
Total cooking time: 15 minutes
Serves 4

olive oil, for cooking
600 g (1¼ lb) chicken breast fillets,
    cut diagonally into thin slices
1 red onion, thinly sliced
3 cloves garlic, finely chopped
2 tablespoons white wine vinegar
1 teaspoon sambal oelek
1 tablespoon lemon juice

12 Kalamata olives, pitted and
    quartered lengthways
¼ cup (40 g/1¼ oz) sun-dried
    tomatoes, cut into thin strips
¼ cup (15 g/½ oz) finely chopped
    fresh parsley
1 tablespoon shredded fresh basil

**1** Heat a wok until very hot, add 2 teaspoons of the oil and swirl it around to coat the side. Stir-fry the chicken slices in two batches until browned and cooked through, adding more oil in between each batch. Remove all the chicken from the wok and keep warm.
**2** Reheat the wok, add 1 tablespoon of the oil and stir-fry the onion until it is soft and golden. Add the garlic and cook for 1 minute. Return the warm chicken to the wok. Add the vinegar, sambal oelek and lemon juice, and toss well.
**3** Stir in the olive pieces, sun-dried tomato, parsley and basil, and season with salt and ground black pepper. Heat through thoroughly.

NUTRITION PER SERVE
Protein 35 g; Fat 15 g; Carbohydrate 2.5 g;
Dietary Fibre 1.5 g; Cholesterol 75 mg;
1420 kJ (335 Cal)

Trim the fat from the chicken breast fillets, and cut into thin diagonal slices.

Sambal oelek is a paste made from salt, vinegar and chilli.

Drain the sun-dried tomatoes and cut them into thin strips.

# GARLIC CALAMARI WITH PARMESAN

Preparation time: 30 minutes +
10 minutes marinating
Total cooking time: 5 minutes
Serves 2–4 (see NOTE)

350 g (11 oz) calamari tubes, cleaned
4 cloves garlic, chopped
2 tablespoons olive oil
2 tablespoons finely chopped fresh
parsley
1 large tomato, peeled, seeded and
finely chopped
1/4 cup (25 g/3/4 oz) grated Parmesan

**1** Cut the calamari tubes in half lengthways, wash and pat dry. Lay them flat, with the soft, fleshy side facing upwards, and cut into rectangular pieces, about 6 x 2.5 cm (2 1/2 x 1 inch). Finely honeycomb by scoring the fleshy side with diagonal strips, one way and then the other, to create a diamond pattern.
**2** Mix the garlic, oil, half the parsley, salt and pepper in a bowl. Add the calamari and refrigerate for at least 10 minutes.
**3** Cook on a very hot, lightly oiled barbecue flatplate in 2 batches, tossing regularly, until they just turn white (take care never to overcook calamari or it can become tough). Add the chopped tomato and toss through to just heat.
**4** Arrange the calamari on a plate and scatter with the Parmesan and remaining parsley.

NUTRITION PER SERVE (4)
Protein 20 g; Fat 15 g; Carbohydrate 2 g;
Dietary Fibre 1 g; Cholesterol 180 mg;
800 kJ (190 cal)

NOTE: This dish will serve four as a starter and two as a main course.

Honeycomb the soft fleshy side of the calamari with a sharp knife.

Combine the garlic, oil, parsley and some salt and pepper in a bowl.

Cook the calamari in batches, tossing regularly, until they turn white.

Serve the calamari topped with a little grated Parmesan and the remaining parsley.

## LAMB WITH EGGPLANT, TOMATO AND PESTO

Preparation time: 30 minutes
Total cooking time: 25 minutes
Serves 4

PESTO
2 cups (100 g/3¹/₂ oz) fresh basil
    leaves
2 cloves garlic, crushed
¹/₃ cup (50 g/1³/₄ oz) pine nuts
³/₄ cup (185 ml/6 fl oz) olive oil
³/₄ cup (75 g/2¹/₂ oz) grated
    Parmesan

1 eggplant
4 Roma tomatoes, halved
6 lamb fillets
60 g (2 oz) goats cheese

**1** To make the pesto, finely chop the basil, garlic and pine nuts in a food processor. With the motor running slowly, gradually pour in the olive oil. Add the Parmesan and process briefly.
**2** Cut the eggplant into thick slices and brush with some olive oil. Cook the eggplant on a hot barbecue grill or flatplate, brushing with a little more oil, for 3–4 minutes each side, or until golden brown and softened. Remove

and keep warm. Add the tomatoes and cook, brushing with olive oil, until soft. Remove and keep warm.
**3** Sprinkle each lamb fillet liberally with black pepper. Wipe the barbecue clean and lightly oil. Cook the lamb for 3–4 minutes, until cooked through but still pink inside. Slice diagonally and serve with the eggplant, tomato and a little pesto. Crumble the goats cheese over the top.

NUTRITION PER SERVE
Protein 35 g; Fat 75 g; Carbohydrate 5 g;
Dietary Fibre 5 g; Cholesterol 95 mg;
3490 kJ (830 cal)

Make the pesto in a food processor, finely chopping the basil, garlic and pine nuts first.

Brush the slices of eggplant with olive oil and then grill until golden brown and softened.

The lamb should be cooked through but still pink inside. Slice diagonally to serve.

# TUNA WITH CAPONATA

Preparation time: 25 minutes + 1 hour
  standing
Total cooking time: 50 minutes
Serves 6

CAPONATA
500 g (1 lb) ripe tomatoes
750 g (1¹/₂ lb) eggplant, diced
¹/₃ cup (80 ml/2³/₄ fl oz) olive oil
2 tablespoons olive oil, extra
1 onion, chopped
3 celery sticks, chopped
2 tablespoons drained capers
¹/₂ cup (90 g/3 oz) green olives, pitted
1 tablespoon sugar
¹/₂ cup (125 ml/4 fl oz) red wine
  vinegar

6 x 200 g (6¹/₂ oz) tuna steaks

**1** To make the caponata, score a cross in the base of each tomato. Place in a bowl of boiling water for 1 minute, then plunge into cold water and peel the skin away from the cross. Cut into small cubes.
**2** Sprinkle the eggplant with salt and leave for 1 hour. Place in a colander, rinse under cold running water and pat dry. Heat the oil in a frying pan and cook the eggplant, in batches, for 4–5 minutes, or until golden and soft. Remove from the pan.
**3** Heat the extra oil in the pan, add the onion and celery, and cook for 3–4 minutes, or until golden. Reduce the heat to low, add the tomato and simmer for 15 minutes, stirring occasionally. Stir in the capers, olives, sugar and vinegar, season and simmer, stirring occasionally, for 10 minutes, or until slightly reduced. Stir in the eggplant. Allow to cool.
**4** Cook the tuna on a hot, lightly oiled barbecue grill or flatplate for 2–3 minutes each side, or until cooked to your liking. Serve immediately with the caponata.

NUTRITION PER SERVE
Protein 45 g; Fat 30 g; Carbohydrate 7 g;
Dietary Fibre 5 g; Cholesterol 140 mg;
1963 kJ (470 cal)

Cook the eggplant, in batches if your pan is small, until golden and soft.

Add the capers, olives, sugar and vinegar to the tomato mixture.

Cook the tuna on a hot barbecue until cooked to your taste.

105

## ITALIAN PORK WITH FENNEL

Preparation time: 15 minutes
Total cooking time: 15 minutes
Serves 4

140 g (4¹/₂ oz) fennel bulb, thinly sliced
oil, for cooking
30 g (1 oz) butter
600 g (1¹/₄ lb) pork fillet, cut into thin strips
1 tablespoon lemon juice
¹/₄ cup (60 ml/2 fl oz) chicken stock

2 tablespoons baby capers, rinsed
Parmesan shavings, to serve
1 tablespoon chopped fennel, to serve

**1** Blanch the fennel in boiling water for 1 minute. Drain and cool under cold running water, then drain again.
**2** Heat the wok until very hot, add 1 tablespoon of the oil and half the butter and swirl it around to coat the side. When the butter begins to sizzle, add the sliced fennel. Stir-fry until golden and tender. Remove from the wok and keep warm.
**3** Reheat the wok, add 2 teaspoons of the oil and half the remaining butter. Stir-fry the pork in two batches until browned, adding more oil and butter between batches. Return the pork and fennel to the wok and add the lemon juice and stock.
**4** Add the capers and stir them through the pork mixture, scraping any bits from the bottom of the wok. Season with salt and pepper, then scatter with the Parmesan and extra fennel. Serve immediately.

NUTRITION PER SERVE
Protein 40 g; Fat 20 g; Carbohydrate 2 g;
Dietary Fibre 1 g; Cholesterol 105 mg;
1525 kJ (365 Cal)

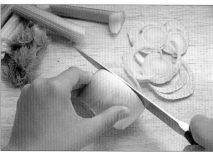

Remove the top from the fennel and thinly slice the bulb.

To make Parmesan shavings, draw a vegetable peeler along the block.

Stir-fry the fennel in the oil and butter until it is golden and tender.

## MEDITERRANEAN CHICKEN SKEWERS

Preparation time: 20 minutes +
  2 hours marinating
Total cooking time: 10 minutes
Makes 8 skewers

32 chicken tenderloins
24 cherry tomatoes
6 cap mushrooms, cut into quarters
2 cloves garlic, crushed
rind of 1 lemon, grated
2 tablespoons lemon juice
2 tablespoons olive oil
1 tablespoon fresh oregano leaves,
  chopped

**1** Soak 8 wooden skewers in water to prevent scorching. Thread a piece of chicken onto each skewer, followed by a tomato, then a piece of mushroom. Repeat three times for each skewer. Put the skewers in a shallow, non-metallic dish.
**2** Combine the garlic, lemon rind, lemon juice, olive oil and chopped oregano, pour over the skewers and toss well. Marinate for at least 2 hours, or overnight if time permits.
**3** Cook the skewers on a hot, lightly oiled barbecue grill or flatplate for 4 minutes on each side, basting occasionally, until the chicken is cooked and the tomatoes have shrivelled slightly.

NUTRITION PER SKEWER
Protein 34 g; Fat 8 g; Carbohydrate 1 g;
Dietary Fibre 1 g; Cholesterol 75 mg;
909 kJ (217 cal)

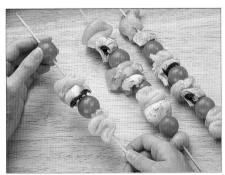

Thread the chicken tenderloins, cherry tomatoes and pieces of mushroom on the skewers.

Put the skewers in a shallow, non-metallic dish and marinate for at least 2 hours.

Cook the skewers for 4 minutes on each side, basting occasionally.

## TUNA WITH MEDITERRANEAN VEGETABLES

Preparation time: 15 minutes +
  30 minutes marinating
Total cooking time: 20 minutes
Serves 4

3/4 cup (185 ml/6 fl oz) olive oil
3 cloves garlic, crushed
2 tablespoons sweet chilli sauce
1 red capsicum, cut into bite-sized
  pieces
1 yellow capsicum, cut into bite-sized
  pieces
2 large zucchini, thickly sliced
2 slender eggplant, thickly sliced
olive oil, extra, for brushing
4 tuna steaks

LEMON AND CAPER MAYONNAISE
1 egg yolk
1 teaspoon grated lemon rind
2 tablespoons lemon juice
1 small clove garlic, chopped
3/4 cup (185 ml/6 fl oz) olive oil
1 tablespoon baby capers

**1** Combine the olive oil, garlic and sweet chilli sauce in a large bowl. Add the capsicum, zucchini and eggplant, toss well, then marinate for 30 minutes.
**2** For the mayonnaise, process the egg yolk, rind, lemon juice and garlic together in a food processor until smooth. With the motor running, gradually add the oil in a thin steady stream until the mixture thickens and is a creamy consistency. Stir in the capers and 1/2 teaspoon salt. Set aside.
**3** Cook the drained vegetables on a hot, lightly oiled barbecue grill or flatplate for 4–5 minutes each side, or until cooked through. Keep warm.

**4** Brush the tuna steaks with the extra oil and barbecue for 2–3 minutes each side, or until just cooked (tuna should be rare in the centre). Serve the vegetables and tuna steaks with the lemon and caper mayonnaise.

NUTRITION PER SERVE
Protein 68 g; Fat 69 g; Carbohydrate 6 g;
Dietary Fibre 3 g; Cholesterol 151 mg;
3885 kJ (925 cal)

VARIATION: This recipe is also suitable for use with Atlantic salmon or swordfish.

Process the mayonnaise ingredients until smooth and creamy.

Turn the vegetables over when browned on one side, then cook through.

## MUSHROOM AND EGGPLANT SKEWERS WITH TOMATO SAUCE

Preparation time: 20 minutes +
 15 minutes marinating
Total cooking time: 30 minutes
Serves 4

12 long fresh rosemary sprigs
18 Swiss brown mushrooms,
 halved
1 small eggplant, cubed
3 tablespoons olive oil
2 tablespoons balsamic vinegar
2 cloves garlic, crushed
1 teaspoon sugar

TOMATO SAUCE
5 tomatoes
1 tablespoon olive oil
1 small onion, finely chopped
1 clove garlic, crushed
1 tablespoon tomato paste
2 teaspoons sugar
2 teaspoons balsamic vinegar
1 tablespoon chopped fresh
 flat-leaf parsley

**1** Remove the leaves from the lower part of the rosemary sprigs. Reserve a tablespoon of the leaves. Put the mushrooms and eggplant in a large non-metallic bowl. Pour on the combined oil, vinegar, garlic and sugar and toss. Marinate for 15 minutes.
**2** To make the tomato sauce, score a cross in the base of each tomato. Put in a bowl of boiling water for 30 seconds, then plunge into cold water. Peel the skin away from the cross. Cut in half and scoop out the seeds with a teaspoon. Dice the flesh.
**3** Heat the oil in a saucepan. Cook the onion and garlic over medium heat for 2–3 minutes, or until soft. Reduce the heat, add the tomato, tomato paste, sugar, vinegar and parsley and simmer for 10 minutes, or until thick.
**4** Thread alternating mushroom halves and eggplant cubes onto the rosemary sprigs. Cook on a hot, lightly oiled barbecue grill or flatplate for 7–8 minutes, or until the eggplant is tender, turning occasionally. Serve with the sauce.

NUTRITION PER SERVE
Protein 3 g; Fat 24 g; Carbohydrate 8.5 g;
Dietary Fibre 4 g; Cholesterol 0 mg;
1100 kJ (263 cal)

Simmer the tomato sauce until the liquid has evaporated and the sauce is thick.

Thread alternating mushrooms and eggplant cubes onto the skewers.

## LAMB CUTLETS WITH PARMESAN POLENTA AND RATATOUILLE

Preparation time: 25 minutes +
  10 minutes cooling
Total cooking time: 2 hours 35 minutes
Serves 4

1 kg (2 lb) lamb bones
1 onion, chopped
1 large carrot, chopped
1 celery stick, chopped
1 bay leaf
1 teaspoon black peppercorns
4 cloves garlic, peeled and bruised
6 Roma tomatoes, chopped
1 cup (250 ml/8 fl oz) red wine
2 cups (500 ml/16 fl oz) sherry
4 sprigs fresh thyme
1 red onion
1 eggplant
1 small red capsicum
1 small green capsicum
1 small yellow capsicum
1 zucchini
1 tablespoon finely chopped fresh
  thyme
2 tablespoons olive oil
1 litre chicken stock
1 cup (170 g/5$\frac{1}{2}$ oz) instant polenta
40 g (1$\frac{1}{4}$ oz) butter
$\frac{1}{2}$ cup (50 g/1$\frac{3}{4}$ oz) finely grated
  Parmesan
2 tablespoons olive oil, for pan-frying,
  extra
12 lamb cutlets
2 tablespoons finely chopped fresh
  parsley

**1** Cook the lamb bones in a saucepan over medium heat, stirring occasionally, for 5 minutes, or until browned. Add the onion, carrot, celery, bay leaf, peppercorns, garlic, tomato, wine, sherry, thyme and 1 litre cold water. Bring to the boil, then reduce the heat and simmer for 2 hours, skimming off any scum. Remove the bones, then strain into a saucepan and simmer for 30 minutes, or until thickened—you should have about $\frac{3}{4}$ cup (185 ml/ 6 fl oz) sauce. Cover and keep warm.

**2** Meanwhile, preheat the oven to moderately hot 200°C (400°F/Gas 6). To make the ratatouille, cut the onion, eggplant, capsicums and zucchini into 1.5 cm (5/8 inch) cubes and combine in a large roasting tin. Add the thyme and drizzle with the oil. Season, then spread in a single layer. Roast, stirring occasionally, for 30–35 minutes, or until just cooked and starting to brown. Remove from the oven and cover with foil. Reduce the heat to moderate 180°C (350°F/Gas 4).

**3** While the ratatouille is cooking, bring the chicken stock to the boil, then slowly pour in the polenta, stirring constantly. Cook, stirring, for 8–10 minutes, or until the polenta is smooth and thick. Stir in the butter and Parmesan. Season and keep warm.

**4** Heat 1 tablespoon of the extra olive oil in a frying pan over high heat and sear the cutlets in batches for 1 minute each side, then place in a single layer in a roasting tin. Bake for 4–5 minutes for a medium-rare result. Remove from the oven, cover and rest for 10 minutes. If necessary, reheat the ratatouille in the oven for 5 minutes. Stir in the parsley just before serving.

**5** To serve, dollop polenta onto each plate, top with three cutlets and some ratatouille. Drizzle with the sauce.

NUTRITION PER SERVE
Protein 35 g; Fat 39 g; Carbohydrate 42 g;
Dietary Fibre 8 g; Cholesterol 105 mg;
3466 kJ (828 Cal)

Cook the lamb bones until they are well browned all over.

Simmer the liquid, skimming off any scum that forms on top.

Simmer the strained liquid in a clean saucepan until just thickened.

Toss the vegetables, thyme and oil together, then cook until just browned.

Cook the polenta, stirring constantly, until it is smooth and thick.

Sear the lamb cutlets in batches for 1 minute each side.

# CALAMARI RINGS WITH SALSA VERDE

Preparation time: 30 minutes +
   30 minutes marinating
Total cooking time: 15 minutes
Serves 4

1 kg (2 lb) calamari
1 cup (250 ml/8 fl oz) olive oil
2 tablespoons lemon juice
2 cloves garlic, crushed
2 tablespoons chopped fresh oregano
2 tablespoons chopped fresh
   flat-leaf parsley
lemon wedges, to serve

SALSA VERDE
2 anchovy fillets, drained
1 tablespoon capers
1 clove garlic, crushed
2 tablespoons chopped fresh
   flat-leaf parsley
2 tablespoons olive oil

1  To clean the calamari, hold onto the hood and gently pull the tentacles away from the head. Cut out the beak and discard with any intestines still attached to the tentacles. Rinse the tentacles in cold running water, pat dry and cut into 5 cm (2 inch) lengths. Place in a bowl. Clean out the hood cavity and remove the transparent backbone. Under cold running water, pull away the skin, rinse and dry well. Cut into rings and place in the bowl with the tentacles. Add the oil, lemon juice, garlic and oregano and toss to coat. Refrigerate for 30 minutes.
2  To make the salsa verde, crush the anchovy fillets in a mortar and pestle. Rinse and chop the capers very finely and mix with the anchovies. Add the garlic and parsley, then slowly stir in the olive oil. Season and mix well.
3  Drain the calamari and cook on a hot, lightly oiled barbecue grill or flatplate in batches for 1–2 minutes each side, basting with the marinade. To serve, sprinkle the calamari with salt, pepper and fresh parsley, and serve with the salsa verde and lemon wedges.

NUTRITION PER SERVE
Protein 42.5 g; Fat 72 g; Carbohydrate 0.5 g;
Dietary Fibre 0.5 g; Cholesterol 499 mg;
3404 kJ (813 cal)

Hold the calamari and gently pull the tentacles away from the head.

Mix together the crushed anchovies, capers, garlic and parsley.

Cook the calamari in batches on a hot barbecue grill or flatplate.

# SWORDFISH SKEWERS WITH WHITE BEAN PUREE

Preparation time: 25 minutes +
   30 minutes soaking +
   30 minutes marinating
Total cooking time: 20 minutes
Serves 4

1 kg (2 lb) swordfish steaks, cut into
   3 cm (1¼ inch) cubes
1 tablespoon olive oil
2 tablespoons lemon juice
1 clove garlic, crushed
1 tablespoon chopped fresh rosemary
1 tablespoon chopped fresh thyme
2 tablespoons chopped fresh
   flat-leaf parsley

WHITE BEAN PURÉE
2 x 400 g (13 oz) cans cannellini beans
1½ cups (375 ml/12 fl oz) chicken
   stock
2 fresh bay leaves
2 cloves garlic, crushed
1 teaspoon chopped fresh thyme
½ teaspoon finely grated lemon rind
¼ cup (60 ml/2 fl oz) extra virgin
   olive oil

**1** Soak eight wooden skewers in water for at least 30 minutes to prevent them from burning during cooking. Thread the swordfish cubes onto the skewers. Place in a large non-metallic dish and pour on the combined olive oil, lemon juice, garlic, rosemary and thyme. Season well. Cover with plastic wrap and refrigerate for at least 30 minutes.
**2** Meanwhile, to make the white bean purée, wash the beans in a colander and place in a large saucepan. Add the chicken stock, bay leaves and ½ cup (125 ml/4 fl oz) water. Bring to the

boil, then reduce the heat and simmer for 10 minutes. Remove from the heat and drain well, reserving 2 tablespoons of the liquid.
**3** Place the beans and the reserved liquid in a food processor or blender with the garlic, thyme and lemon rind. Season with salt and freshly ground black pepper and process until smooth. With the motor running, gradually pour in the olive oil in a thin stream. Continue processing until well combined, then keep warm.

**4** Heat a chargrill or hot plate until very hot. Cook the skewers, turning regularly and basting with any leftover marinade, for 3–4 minutes, or until cooked through and golden.
**5** Serve the skewers warm, sprinkled with parsley and a spoonful of white bean purée on the side.

NUTRITION PER SERVE
Protein 62 g; Fat 21 g; Carbohydrate 18 g;
Dietary Fibre 9 g; Cholesterol 147 mg;
2115 kJ (505 Cal)

Drain the beans over a heatproof bowl and reserve some of the liquid.

Process the beans, garlic, thyme and lemon rind, then the oil, in a food processor.

Chargrill the swordfish skewers until cooked through and golden.

## POLENTA WITH WILD MUSHROOMS

Preparation time: 30 minutes + chilling
Total cooking time: 1 hour 20 minutes
Serves 6–8

2¹/₂ cups (600 ml/20 fl oz) vegetable stock
2 cups (300 g/10 oz) polenta
100 g (3¹/₂ oz) Parmesan, grated

MUSHROOM SAUCE
1 kg (2 lb) mixed mushrooms (roman, oyster and flat)
¹/₂ cup (125 ml/4 fl oz) olive oil
¹/₂ cup (15 g/¹/₂ oz) chopped parsley
4 cloves garlic, finely chopped
1 onion, chopped

**1** Put the stock and 2 cups (500 ml/16 fl oz) water in a large pan and bring to the boil. Add the polenta and stir constantly for 10 minutes until very thick. Remove from the heat and stir in the Parmesan. Brush a 20 cm (8 inch) round springform tin with oil. Spread the polenta into the tin and smooth the surface. Refrigerate for 2 hours, turn out and cut into 6–8 wedges.
**2** To make the sauce, wipe the mushrooms with a damp cloth and roughly chop the larger ones. Put the mushrooms, oil, parsley, garlic and onion in a pan. Stir, cover and leave to simmer for 50 minutes, or until cooked through. Uncover and cook for 10 minutes, or until there is very little liquid left. Set aside.
**3** Brush one side of the polenta with oil and cook under a preheated grill (broiler) for 5 minutes, or until the edges are browned. Turn over and brown. Reheat the mushroom sauce and serve spooned over slices of polenta.

NUTRITION PER SERVE (6)
Protein 11 g; Fat 20 g; Carbohydrate 11 g; Dietary Fibre 4 g; Cholesterol 12 mg; 1103 kJ (214 cal)

Stir the polenta until very thick, remove from the heat and add the Parmesan.

Refrigerate the tin of polenta for 2 hours, then turn out and cut into wedges.

Uncover the mushrooms and let them simmer for 10 minutes, until little liquid is left.

# CHICKEN WITH ROASTED RED CAPSICUM SAUCE

Preparation time: 30 minutes
Total cooking time: 1 hour 15 minutes
Serves 4
Fat per serve: 7.5 g

2 red capsicums
1 tablespoon olive oil
1 red onion, roughly chopped
1–2 cloves garlic, crushed
425 g (14 oz) can chopped tomatoes
1/2 cup (30 g/1 oz) chopped fresh
    parsley
1/2 cup (30 g/1 oz) chopped fresh
    basil leaves
1 tablespoon tomato paste
1 tablespoon caster sugar
4 chicken breast fillets

**1** Cut the capsicums into quarters, remove the membrane and seeds and grill, skin-side-up, until blackened. Cool in a plastic bag for 10 minutes, peel away the skin and chop roughly.
**2** Heat the oil in a pan and cook the onion and garlic for 2 minutes, or until soft but not brown. Add the tomatoes, parsley, basil, tomato paste, sugar and 1 1/2 cups (375 ml/12 fl oz) water.
**3** Add the chopped capsicum and cook, stirring often, over very low heat for 45 minutes to 1 hour, or until thick. Leave to cool slightly, then purée in batches in a food processor. Season.
**4** Cook the chicken in a frying pan for 5 minutes on each side, or until cooked through and tender. Serve with the sauce.

NUTRITION PER SERVE
Protein 27 g; Fat 7.5 g; Carbohydrate 9 g;
Dietary Fibre 2 g; Cholesterol 55 mg;
886 kJ (210 cal)

Once the capsicum skin has been blackened it should peel away easily.

Cook the onion and garlic until they are softened but not browned.

Add the chopped capsicum to the sauce and cook for up to 1 hour, or until thick.

## BARBECUED TUNA AND WHITE BEAN SALAD

Preparation time: 25 minutes
Total cooking time: 5 minutes
Serves 4–6

400 g (13 oz) tuna steaks
1 small red onion, thinly sliced
1 tomato, seeded and chopped
1 small red capsicum, thinly sliced
2 x 400 g (13 oz) cans cannellini
    beans
2 cloves garlic, crushed
1 teaspoon chopped fresh thyme
4 tablespoons finely chopped fresh
    flat-leaf parsley

1½ tablespoons lemon juice
⅓ cup (80 ml/2¾ fl oz) extra virgin
    olive oil
1 teaspoon honey
100 g (3½ oz) rocket leaves

**1** Place the tuna steaks on a plate, sprinkle with cracked black pepper on both sides, cover with plastic and refrigerate until needed.
**2** Combine the onion, tomato and capsicum in a large bowl. Rinse the cannellini beans under cold running water for 30 seconds, drain and add to the bowl with the garlic, thyme and 3 tablespoons of the parsley.
**3** Place the lemon juice, oil and honey in a small pan, bring to the boil, then

simmer, stirring, for 1 minute, or until the honey dissolves. Remove from the heat.
**4** Cook the tuna on a hot, lightly oiled barbecue grill or flatplate for 1 minute on each side. The meat should still be pink in the middle. Slice into small cubes and combine with the salad. Toss with the warm dressing.
**5** Arrange the rocket on a platter. Top with the salad, season well and toss with the remaining parsley.

NUTRITION PER SERVE (6)
Protein 30 g; Fat 20 g; Carbohydrate 17 g;
Dietary Fibre 10 g; Cholesterol 0 mg;
1656 kJ (394 cal)

Add the beans, garlic, thyme and parsley to the bowl and mix well.

Heat the lemon juice, honey and oil in a saucepan until the honey dissolves.

Cook the tuna until still pink in the middle and cut into small cubes.

# CHICKEN WITH LEMON AND CAPERS

Preparation time: 15 minutes
Total cooking time: 15 minutes
Serves 4

olive oil, for cooking
1 red onion, cut into thin wedges
25 g (3/4 oz) butter
800 g (1 lb 10 oz) chicken breast
    fillets, cut into bite-sized pieces
rind of 1 lemon, cut into thin strips
2 tablespoons baby capers, rinsed
    well and drained
1/3 cup (80 ml/2 3/4 fl oz) lemon juice
1/4 cup (15 g/1/2 oz) shredded fresh
    basil

**1** Heat the wok until very hot, add 2 teaspoons of the oil and swirl it around to coat the side. Add the red onion wedges and stir-fry until softened and golden. Remove from the wok and set aside.
**2** Reheat the wok, add 2 teaspoons of the oil and half the butter, and stir-fry the chicken in two batches until it is browned, adding more oil and butter between batches. Return all the chicken to the wok with the onion.
**3** Stir in the lemon rind, capers and lemon juice. Toss well and cook until warmed through. Add the shredded basil and season with salt and black pepper. Delicious served with creamy mashed potato.

NUTRITION PER SERVE
Protein 45 g; Fat 20 g; Carbohydrate 2.5 g;
Dietary Fibre 1 g; Cholesterol 115 mg;
1550 kJ (370 Cal)

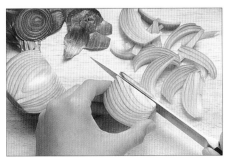

Peel the red onion, then cut it in half and cut it into thin wedges.

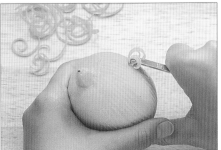

Use a zester to remove thin strips of rind from the lemon, without getting the pith from underneath.

Stir-fry the red onion wedges until they are soft and golden.

from the oven

## LAMB CASSEROLE WITH BEANS

Preparation time: 25 minutes +
  overnight soaking
Total cooking time: 2 hours 15 minutes
Serves 6

1½ cups (300 g/10 oz) borlotti beans
  or red kidney beans
1 kg (2 lb) boned leg lamb
1½ tablespoons olive oil
2 rashers bacon, rind removed,
  chopped
1 large onion, chopped
2 cloves garlic, crushed
1 large carrot, chopped
2 cups (500 ml/16 oz) dry red wine
1 tablespoon tomato paste

1½ cups (375 ml/12 fl oz) beef stock
2 large sprigs fresh rosemary
2 sprigs fresh thyme

**1** Put the beans in a bowl and cover with plenty of water. Leave to soak overnight, then drain well.
**2** Preheat the oven to warm 160°C (315°F/Gas 2–3). Trim any excess fat from the lamb and cut into 3 cm (1¼ inch) pieces.
**3** Heat 1 tablespoon oil in a large flameproof casserole. Add half the meat and toss over medium–high heat for 2 minutes, or until browned. Remove from the pan and repeat with the remaining lamb.
**4** Heat the remaining olive oil in the casserole and add the bacon and onion. Cook over medium heat for

3 minutes, or until the onion is translucent. Add the garlic and carrot, and cook for 1 minute, or until aromatic.
**5** Return the meat and any juices to the pan, increase the heat to high and add the wine. Bring to the boil and cook for 2 minutes. Add the beans, tomato paste, stock, rosemary and thyme, bring to the boil, then cover and cook in the oven for 2 hours, or until the meat is tender. Stir occasionally during cooking. Skim off any excess fat, remove the sprigs of herbs and season. Serve with bread.

NUTRITION PER SERVE
Protein 50 g; Fat 10 g; Carbohydrate 48 g;
Dietary Fibre 9 g; Cholesterol 117 mg;
2367 kJ (565 Cal)

Remove any excess fat from the lamb then cut it into 3 cm (1¼ inch) pieces.

Heat the oil then add the lamb and toss until browned all over.

Return the meat and juices to the pan, add the wine, and bring to the boil.

# MEDITERRANEAN PIE

Preparation time: 25 minutes +
 20 minutes refrigeration
Total cooking time: 35 minutes
Serves 4

3 cups (375 g/12 oz) plain flour
1 egg, lightly beaten
1/2 cup (125 ml/4 fl oz) buttermilk
100 ml (31/2 fl oz) olive oil

FILLING
2 tablespoons olive oil
100 g (31/2 oz) button mushrooms,
 sliced
400 g (13 oz) can tomatoes, drained
 and roughly chopped
100 g (31/2 oz) sliced salami
180 g (6 oz) jar artichokes, drained
4 tablespoons fresh basil leaves, torn
100 g (31/2 oz) mozzarella, grated
1/4 cup (30 g/1 oz) grated Parmesan
milk, to brush

**1** Preheat the oven to hot 210°C
(415°F/Gas 6–7). Grease a large baking
tray and place in the oven to heat up.
Sift the flour into a large bowl and add

the egg and buttermilk. Add the oil
and mix with a large metal spoon until
the mixture comes together and forms
a soft dough (add a little water if the
mixture is too dry). Turn onto a lightly
floured surface and gather together
into a smooth ball. Cover with plastic
wrap and refrigerate for 20 minutes.
**2** Heat the oil in a large frying pan,
add the button mushrooms and cook
over medium heat for 5 minutes, or
until they have softened and browned
a little.
**3** Divide the pastry in half and roll
each portion, between two sheets of
baking paper, into a 30 cm (12 inch)
round. Layer the chopped tomato,
salami, mushrooms, artichokes, basil

leaves, mozzarella and Parmesan
on one of the pastry rounds, leaving
a narrow border. Season well.
**4** Brush the border with milk. Top
with the remaining pastry circle to
enclose the filling, then pinch and
seal the edges together. Make three
slits in the top. Brush the top with
milk. Place on the preheated tray and
bake for 30 minutes, or until golden.

NUTRITION PER SERVE
Protein 30 g; Fat 52 g; Carbohydrate 75 g;
Dietary Fibre 7 g; Cholesterol 95 mg;
3675 kJ (880 Cal)

Gently gather the dough together to form a
smooth ball.

Brush the pastry border with milk to help the top
layer of pastry stick.

# MEDITERRANEAN CHICKEN

Preparation time: 30 minutes
Total cooking time: 1 hour 10 minutes
Serves 4

8 chicken thigh cutlets
2 tablespoons olive oil
150 g (5 oz) French shallots
4 cloves garlic
1/2 cup (125 ml/4 fl oz) white wine
425 g (14 oz) can chopped tomatoes
12 Kalamata olives
1 tablespoon red wine vinegar
2 teaspoons tomato paste
1 tablespoon fresh oregano leaves
1 tablespoon chopped fresh basil
1 teaspoon sugar
4 slices prosciutto
1 teaspoon grated lemon rind
1/2 cup (30 g/1 oz) chopped fresh
    parsley
1 tablespoon capers, rinsed

**1** Preheat the oven to moderate 180°C (350°F/Gas 4). Remove the skin and fat from the chicken thighs. Heat half the oil in a large pan and brown the chicken over high heat for 3–4 minutes on each side. Arrange the chicken in a large flameproof casserole dish.

**2** Heat the remaining oil in the same pan. Add the shallots and garlic and cook over medium heat for 4 minutes, or until soft but not brown. Add the wine and bring to the boil.

**3** Add the tomatoes, olives, vinegar, tomato paste, oregano, basil and sugar. Season with salt and black pepper. Boil, stirring, for 2 minutes, then pour over the chicken and cover with a tight-fitting lid. Bake for 45 minutes, or until the chicken is tender.

**4** Meanwhile, place the prosciutto in a single layer in a frying pan. Dry-fry for 3 minutes, or until crisp, turning once. Break into large chunks and set aside.

**5** Arrange the chicken on a serving dish, cover and keep warm. Transfer the casserole to the stove top and boil the pan juices for 5 minutes, or until thickened, stirring occasionally. Spoon the juices over the chicken and sprinkle with the lemon rind, parsley and capers. Top with the prosciutto.

NUTRITION PER SERVE
Protein 75 g; Fat 25 g; Carbohydrate 15 g;
Dietary Fibre 8 g; Cholesterol 155 mg;
2390 kJ (570 cal)

Cook the shallots and garlic until soft, then add the wine.

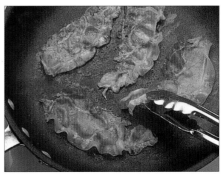

Place the prosciutto slices in a single layer in a dry frying pan and fry until crisp.

# STUFFED ZUCCHINI

Preparation time: 20 minutes
Total cooking time: 45 minutes
Serves 4

8 zucchini
35 g (1¼ oz) white bread, crusts
    removed
milk, for soaking
125 g (4 oz) ricotta cheese
3 tablespoons grated Cheddar cheese
¹/₃ cup (35 g/1¼ oz) grated
    Parmesan

2 teaspoons chopped fresh oregano
2 teaspoons chopped fresh thyme
1 clove garlic, crushed
1 egg yolk

**1** Preheat the oven to moderately hot
190°C (375°F/Gas 5). Cook the
zucchini in boiling salted water for
5 minutes, then drain. Meanwhile,
soak the bread in milk until soft, then
squeeze dry. Cut the zucchini in half
and scoop out the flesh with a spoon.
**2** Chop the zucchini flesh finely. Place
in a bowl and add the bread, cheeses,
herbs, garlic, egg yolk and season with

salt and pepper. Mix together, adding a
little milk to make it bind if necessary.
**3** Fill the zucchini shells with the
stuffing. Brush an ovenproof baking
dish with oil and arrange the zucchini
close together. Bake in the oven for
35–40 minutes, until golden on top.
Serve immediately.

NUTRITION PER SERVE
Protein 12 g; Fat 10 g; Carbohydrate 10 g;
Dietary Fibre 4.5 g; Cholesterol 73 mg;
758 kJ (180 cal)

Cut the zucchini in half and scoop out the flesh
with a teaspoon.

Combine the zucchini, cheeses, herbs,
garlic and egg yolk in a bowl.

Arrange the stuffed zucchini close together in the
oiled baking dish.

# ROMAN GNOCCHI

Preparation time: 15 minutes +
  1 hour refrigeration
Total cooking time: 40 minutes
Serves 4

3 cups (750 ml/24 fl oz) milk
1/2 teaspoon ground nutmeg
3/4 cup (90 g/3 oz) semolina
1 egg, beaten
1 1/2 cups (150 g/5 oz) grated
  Parmesan
60 g (2 oz) butter, melted
1/2 cup (125 ml/4 fl oz) cream
1/2 cup (60 g/2 oz) grated mozzarella

**1** Line a deep 30 x 20 cm (12 x 8 inch) swiss roll tin with baking paper. Put the milk, half the nutmeg and some salt and pepper in a pan and bring to the boil. Reduce the heat and gradually stir in the semolina. Cook, stirring occasionally, for 5–10 minutes or until the semolina is very stiff.
**2** Remove from the heat. Add the egg and 1 cup (100 g/3 1/2 oz) Parmesan and stir well. Spread into the tin and refrigerate for 1 hour or until firm.
**3** Preheat the oven to moderate 180°C (350°F/Gas 4). Cut the semolina into rounds with a floured 4 cm (1 1/2 inch) cutter. Arrange in a greased shallow casserole dish.

**4** Pour the butter over the top and then the cream. Sprinkle with the combined remaining Parmesan and mozzarella cheeses. Sprinkle with the remaining nutmeg. Bake for 20–25 minutes or until golden.

NUTRITION PER SERVE
Protein 33 g; Fat 53 g; Carbohydrate 24 g;
Dietary Fibre 0.5 g; Cholesterol 205 mg;
2918 kJ (697 cal)

NOTE: Roman gnocchi is also known as gnocchi alla semolina, to differentiate it from the small potato gnocchi that are boiled and served with pasta sauce.

Cook the semolina for 5–10 minutes, or until it is very stiff.

Use a floured biscuit cutter to cut the gnocchi into circles.

Mix together the grated Parmesan and mozzarella and sprinkle over the gnocchi.

## PARMESAN AND PROSCIUTTO LOAF

Preparation time: 30 minutes + 2 hours rising
Total cooking time: 25 minutes
Serves 6

7 g (¹/4 oz) dried yeast
1 teaspoon caster sugar
¹/2 cup (125 ml/4 fl oz) warm milk
2 cups (250 g/8 oz) plain flour
1 teaspoon salt
1 egg, lightly beaten
30 g (1 oz) butter, melted and cooled slightly
1 tablespoon milk, extra

60 g (2 oz) sliced prosciutto, finely chopped
¹/2 cup (50 g/1³/4 oz) grated Parmesan

**1** Mix the yeast, sugar and milk in a bowl. Cover and set aside in a warm place for 10 minutes, or until frothy.
**2** Mix the flour and salt in a bowl. Make a well in the centre and add the egg, butter and frothy yeast. Mix to a soft dough and gather into a ball; turn out onto a floured surface and knead for 8 minutes, or until elastic.
**3** Put in an oiled bowl, cover loosely with greased plastic wrap and leave in a warm place for 1¹/4 hours, or until doubled in size.

**4** Punch down the dough, turn out onto a floured surface and knead for 30 seconds, or until smooth. Roll out to a rectangle, 30 x 20 cm (12 x 8 inches), and brush with some extra milk. Sprinkle with the prosciutto and Parmesan, leaving a border. Roll lengthways into a log shape.
**5** Lay on a greased baking tray and brush with the remaining milk. Slash the loaf at intervals. Leave to rise in a warm place for 30 minutes. Bake at 220°C (425°F/Gas 7) for 25 minutes.

NUTRITION PER SERVE
Protein 10 g; Fat 9 g; Carbohydrate 30 g; Dietary Fibre 2 g; Cholesterol 60 mg; 1060 kJ (250 cal)

Sprinkle the prosciutto and Parmesan on the dough, leaving a clear border.

Roll up the dough tightly lengthways into a log shape for baking.

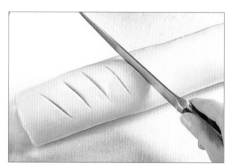

Using a sharp knife, slash the loaf diagonally at intervals.

126

# CHARGRILLED VEGETABLE PIE WITH POLENTA PASTRY

Preparation time: 1 hour +
  50 minutes refrigeration
Total cooking time: 55 minutes
Serves 4–6

POLENTA PASTRY
1 cup (125 g/4 oz) plain flour
1/2 cup (75 g/2 1/2 oz) polenta
90 g (3 oz) cold butter, cubed
90 g (3 oz) cream cheese, cubed

1 kg (2 lb) eggplant, sliced lengthways
2 large tablespoons olive oil
1–2 cloves garlic, crushed
2 red capsicums, halved and seeded
8 cherry tomatoes, halved
handful of small basil leaves
2 teaspoons baby capers
1 teaspoon balsamic vinegar
1 teaspoon olive oil, extra

**1** Place the flour, polenta, butter and cream cheese in a food processor. Process in short bursts until the mixture just comes together. Add 1–2 teaspoons of cold water if needed. Turn out onto a floured surface and quickly bring together into a ball. Cover with plastic wrap and refrigerate for at least 30 minutes.
**2** Brush the eggplant with the combined olive oil and garlic and grill or barbecue for 10–12 minutes, turning once and brushing 2–3 times during cooking. Cook the capsicum, skin-side-up, for 5–8 minutes, until the skin has blackened. Cool in a plastic bag, remove the skin and slice. Cook the tomatoes, cut-side-up, for 2–3 minutes.
**3** Roll out the pastry on baking paper to fit a shallow 21 x 28 cm

(8 1/2 x 11 inch) loose-based flan tin. Press well into the sides and trim off any excess. Refrigerate for 20 minutes. Preheat the oven to moderately hot 190°C (375°F/Gas 5). Cover the pastry shell with baking paper and fill with baking beads. Bake for 15 minutes. Remove the paper and beads and bake the pastry shell for 15 minutes, or until it is cooked.

**4** Layer the pastry with capsicum, eggplant, tomato halves, some basil leaves and capers. Brush with the combined balsamic vinegar and oil before serving.

NUTRITION PER SERVE (6)
Protein 7 g; Fat 25 g; Carbohydrate 30 g;
Dietary Fibre 6 g; Cholesterol 55 mg;
1600 kJ (380 cal)

Crush the garlic; halve and seed the capsicums and halve the cherry tomatoes.

Process the mixture in short bursts until it just comes together.

Roll out the pastry on a sheet of baking paper until large enough to fit the tin.

127

# SPINACH AND RICOTTA LATTICE TART

Preparation time: 50 minutes +
 15 minutes refrigeration
Total cooking time: 50 minutes
Serves 6

2 cups (250 g/8 oz) plain flour
125 g (4 oz) butter, chilled and cubed
1 egg
2 tablespoons sesame seeds
2–3 tablespoons iced water

SPINACH AND RICOTTA FILLING
50 g (1³/4 oz) butter
1 cup (125 g/4 oz) finely chopped
 spring onions
2 cloves garlic, crushed
500 g (1 lb) English spinach, trimmed,
 washed and roughly shredded
2 tablespoons chopped fresh mint
³/4 cup (185 g/6 oz) ricotta cheese
¹/2 cup (50 g/1³/4 oz) grated
 Parmesan
3 eggs, beaten
1–2 tablespoons milk

**1** Place the flour and butter in a food processor and process for 15 seconds, or until the mixture resembles fine breadcrumbs. Add the egg, sesame seeds and water. Process in short bursts until the mixture just comes together, adding a little extra water if necessary. Turn out onto a lightly floured surface and quickly gather into a ball. Cover the pastry with plastic wrap and refrigerate for at least 15 minutes. Place a baking tray in the oven and preheat the oven to 180°C (350°F/Gas 4).
**2** To make the filling, melt the butter in a large pan, add the spring onions and garlic and cook until soft. Add the spinach a little at a time, then stir in the mint. Remove from the heat and allow to cool slightly before stirring in the ricotta, Parmesan and the beaten eggs. Season and mix well.
**3** Grease a shallow 23 cm (9 inch) loose-based tart tin. Take two-thirds of the pastry and, on a sheet of baking paper, roll it out thinly to line the tin, pressing it well into the sides. Fill the pastry shell with the spinach and ricotta filling.
**4** Roll out the remaining pastry and cut into 1.5 cm (⁵/8 inch) strips. Interweave the pastry strips in a lattice pattern over the top of the tart. Dampen the edge of the pastry base and gently press the strips down. Trim the edges of the pastry by pressing down with your thumb or by rolling a rolling pin across the top of the tin. Brush with milk. Place on the baking tray and bake for about 40 minutes, or until the pastry is golden.

NUTRITION PER SERVE
Protein 20 g; Fat 35 g; Carbohydrate 35 g;
Dietary Fibre 5 g; Cholesterol 215 mg;
2220 kJ (530 cal)

NOTE: Depending on how thick you like to roll your pastry, there may be about 100 g (3¹/2 oz) of pastry trimmings left over. It is easier to have this little bit extra when making the lattice strips as they will be long enough to cover the top of the pie. The extra pastry can be covered and frozen for future use as decorations, or made into small tart shells.

Wash spinach very thoroughly as it can be gritty, then trim and roughly shred.

Allow the filling mixture to cool a little before adding the cheeses and egg.

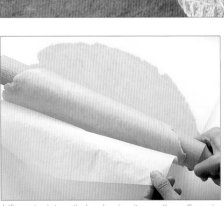

Lift pastry into a tin by draping it over the rolling pin and removing the paper.

Roll out the remaining pastry and cut into thin strips for the lattice.

Interweave the lattice strips over the top of the spinach and ricotta filling.

Dampen the edge of the pastry shell, press down the lattice and trim.

# TOMATO HERB ROLLS

Preparation time: 30 minutes
  + 1 hour 25 minutes rising
Total cooking time: 35 minutes
Makes 12 rolls

7 g (¹⁄₄ oz) dried yeast
1 teaspoon sugar
4 cups (500 g/l lb) plain flour
1 teaspoon salt
2 cloves garlic, finely chopped
¹⁄₂ cup (75 g/2¹⁄₂ oz) sun-dried
  tomatoes, finely chopped
1 tablespoon chopped fresh oregano
1 tablespoon chopped fresh marjoram
1 tablespoon chopped fresh thyme

2 tablespoons chopped fresh flat-leaf
  parsley
30 g (1 oz) butter, melted
¹⁄₂ cup (125 ml/4 fl oz) milk, plus
  extra, to glaze

**1** Mix the yeast, sugar and ¹⁄₂ cup
(125 ml/4 fl oz) of warm water in a
bowl. Set aside for 10 minutes, or until
frothy. Sift the flour and salt into a
bowl and make a well in the centre.
**2** Mix in the garlic, sun-dried tomato
and herbs. Pour in the melted butter,
frothy yeast and milk and mix to a soft
dough. Knead on a lightly floured
surface for 10 minutes, or until
smooth. Cover loosely with greased
plastic wrap and leave for 45 minutes,

or until well risen.
**3** Punch down and knead for
5 minutes. Divide into twelve and roll
into balls. Lay apart on a greased
baking tray. Leave for 30 minutes, or
until well risen. Preheat the oven to
hot 210°C (415°F/Gas 6–7). Brush
the rolls with milk and bake for
10 minutes. Reduce the oven to
180°C (350°F/Gas 4) and bake for
20–25 minutes, or until golden.

NUTRITION PER ROLL
Protein 5 g; Fat 3 g; Carbohydrate 30 g;
Dietary Fibre 2 g; Cholesterol 8 mg;
730 kJ (175 cal)

Add the garlic, sun-dried tomato and herbs to the
flour mixture.

Using a sharp floured knife, divide the dough into
12 equal portions.

The rolls are cooked when the bases sound
hollow when tapped.

# CHICKEN WITH BAKED EGGPLANT AND TOMATO

Preparation time: 30 minutes
Total cooking time: 1 hour 30 minutes
Serves 4

1 red capsicum
1 eggplant
3 tomatoes, cut into quarters
200 g (6½ oz) large button
   mushrooms, halved
1 onion, cut into thin wedges
cooking oil spray
1½ tablespoons tomato paste
½ cup (125 ml/4 fl oz) chicken stock
¼ cup (60 ml/2 fl oz) white wine

2 lean slices bacon
4 chicken breast fillets
4 small fresh rosemary sprigs

**1** Preheat the oven to moderately hot 200°C (400°F/Gas 6). Cut the capsicum and eggplant into bite-sized pieces and combine with the tomato, mushrooms and onion in a baking dish. Spray with oil and bake for 1 hour, or until starting to brown and soften, stirring once.
**2** Pour the combined tomato paste, stock and wine into the dish and bake for 10 minutes, or until thickened.
**3** Meanwhile, discard the fat and rind from the bacon and cut in half. Wrap a strip of bacon around each chicken

breast and secure it underneath with a toothpick. Poke a sprig of fresh rosemary underneath the bacon. Pan-fry in a lightly oiled, non-stick frying pan over medium heat until golden on both sides. Cover and cook for 10–15 minutes, or until the chicken is tender and cooked through. Remove the toothpicks. Serve the chicken on the vegetable mixture, surrounded with the sauce.

NUTRITION PER SERVE
Protein 35 g; Fat 4.5 g; Carbohydrate 8 g; Dietary Fibre 5 g; Cholesterol 70 mg; 965 kJ (230 Cal)

Spray the vegetables lightly with the cooking oil before baking.

When the vegetables have softened, add the combined tomato paste, stock and wine.

Wrap a strip of bacon around the chicken and secure underneath with a toothpick.

# EGGPLANT PARMIGIANA

Preparation time: 30 minutes
Total cooking time: 1 hour 15 minutes
Serves 6–8

3 tablespoons olive oil
1 onion, diced
2 cloves garlic, crushed
1.25 kg (2¹/₂ lb) tomatoes, peeled and
    chopped
1 kg (2 lb) eggplants
250 g (8 oz) bocconcini, sliced
185 g (6 oz) Cheddar cheese, finely
    grated
1 cup (50 g/1³/₄ oz) basil leaves
¹/₂ cup (50 g/1³/₄ oz) grated
    Parmesan

**1** Heat the oil in a large frying pan; add the onion and cook over moderate heat until soft. Add the garlic and cook for 1 minute. Add the tomato and simmer for 15 minutes. Season with salt to taste. Preheat the oven to moderately hot 200°C (400°F/Gas 6).

**2** Slice the eggplants very thinly and shallow-fry in oil in batches for 3–4 minutes, or until golden brown. Drain on paper towels.

**3** Place one third of the eggplant in a 7-cup (1.75 litre) ovenproof dish. Top with half the bocconcini and Cheddar. Repeat the layers, finishing with a layer of eggplant.

**4** Pour the tomato mixture over the eggplant. Scatter with torn basil leaves, then Parmesan. Bake for 40 minutes.

NUTRITION PER SERVE (6)
Protein 19 g; Fat 28 g; Carbohydrate 7 g;
Dietary Fibre 5 g; Cholesterol 60 mg;
1495 kJ (357 cal)

VARIATION: If you prefer not to fry the eggplant, brush it lightly with oil and brown lightly under a hot grill.

Shallow-fry the eggplant in batches, then drain on paper towels.

Arrange layers of eggplant, bocconcini and Cheddar in the dish.

# ARTICHOKE AND PROVOLONE QUICHES

Preparation time: 40 minutes +
  30 minutes refrigeration
Total cooking time: 35 minutes
Serves 6

2 cups (250 g/8 oz) plain flour
125 g (4 oz) cold butter, chopped
1 egg yolk

FILLING
1 small eggplant, sliced
6 eggs, lightly beaten
3 teaspoons wholegrain mustard

150 g (5 oz) provolone cheese, grated
200 g (6½ oz) marinated artichokes,
  sliced
125 g (4 oz) semi-dried tomatoes

**1** Process the flour and butter in a
processor for about 15 seconds until
crumbly. Add the egg yolk and
3 tablespoons of water. Process in
short bursts until the mixture comes
together. Add a little extra water if you
think the dough is a bit too dry. Turn
out onto a floured surface and gather
into a ball. Cover with plastic wrap
and refrigerate for at least 30 minutes.
**2** Preheat the oven to moderately hot
190°C (375°F/Gas 5) and grease six

11 cm (4½ inch) oval pie tins.
**3** To make the filling, brush the sliced
eggplant with olive oil and place
under a grill until golden. Combine the
eggs, mustard and cheese in a jug.
**4** Roll out the pastry and line the tins.
Trim away the excess pastry and
decorate the edges. Place one
eggplant slice and a few artichokes
and tomatoes in each tin, pour the
egg mixture over the top and bake for
25 minutes, or until golden.

NUTRITION PER QUICHE
Protein 20 g; Fat 30 g; Carbohydrate 35 g;
Dietary Fibre 4 g; Cholesterol 290 mg;
2025 kJ (480 cal)

Gather the pastry into a ball and cover with plastic wrap to refrigerate.

Brush each slice of eggplant with a little olive oil and then grill until golden.

Place one slice of eggplant in the bottom of each lined pie tin.

## SUMMER POTATO PIZZA

Preparation time: 30 minutes +
   10 minutes soaking yeast
Total cooking time: 40 minutes
Serves 6

7 g (1/4 oz) sachet dry yeast
2 1/2 cups (310 g/10 oz) plain flour
2 teaspoons polenta or semolina
2 tablespoons olive oil
2 cloves garlic, crushed
4–5 potatoes, unpeeled, thinly sliced
1 tablespoon fresh rosemary leaves

**1** Preheat the oven to hot 210°C
(415°F/Gas 6–7). Combine the yeast,
1/2 teaspoon of salt and sugar and
1 cup (250 ml/8 fl oz) of warm water
in a bowl. Cover and leave in a warm
place for 10 minutes, or until foamy.
Sift the flour into a bowl, make a well
in the centre, add the yeast mixture
and mix to a dough.
**2** Turn the dough out onto a lightly
floured surface and knead for
5 minutes, or until smooth and elastic.
Roll out to a 30 cm (12 inch) circle.
Lightly spray a pizza tray with oil and
sprinkle with polenta or semolina.

**3** Place the pizza base on the tray. Mix
2 teaspoons of the oil with the garlic
and brush over the pizza base. Gently
toss the remaining olive oil, potato
slices, rosemary leaves, 1 teaspoon
of salt and some pepper in a bowl.
**4** Arrange the potato slices in
overlapping circles over the pizza
base and bake for 40 minutes, or
until the base is crisp and golden.

NUTRITION PER SERVE
Protein 9 g; Fat 10 g; Carbohydrate 50 g;
Dietary Fibre 4 g; Cholesterol 0 mg;
1415 kJ (340 Cal)

Leave the yeast mixture in a warm place until it
becomes foamy—this shows it is active.

Knead the dough until firm and elastic, then roll
out to fit a pizza tray.

Brush the dough base with garlic oil, then top
with a layer of potato slices.

# VEGETABLE TART WITH SALSA VERDE

Preparation time: 30 minutes +
    30 minutes refrigeration
Total cooking time: 50 minutes
Serves 6

1³/4 cups (215 g/7 oz) plain flour
120 g (4 oz) chilled butter, cubed
1/4 cup (60 ml/2 fl oz) cream
1–2 tablespoons chilled water
1 large (250 g/8 oz) Desiree potato,
    cut into 2 cm (1 inch) cubes
1 tablespoon olive oil
2 cloves garlic, crushed
1 red capsicum, cut into cubes
1 red onion, sliced into rings
2 zucchini, sliced
2 tablespoons chopped fresh dill
1 tablespoon chopped fresh thyme
1 tablespoon drained baby capers
150 g (5 oz) marinated quartered
    artichoke hearts, drained
2/3 cup (30 g/1 oz) baby English
    spinach leaves

SALSA VERDE
1 clove garlic
2 cups (40 g/1¹/4 oz) fresh flat-leaf
    parsley
1/3 cup (80 ml/2³/4 fl oz) extra virgin
    olive oil
3 tablespoons chopped fresh dill
1¹/2 tablespoons Dijon mustard
1 tablespoon red wine vinegar
1 tablespoon drained baby capers

**1** Sift the flour and 1/2 teaspoon salt into a large bowl. Add the butter and rub it into the flour with your fingertips until it resembles fine breadcrumbs. Add the cream and water and mix with a flat-bladed knife until the mixture comes together in beads. Gather together and lift onto a lightly floured work surface. Press into a ball, then flatten into a disc, wrap in plastic wrap and refrigerate for 30 minutes.

**2** Preheat the oven to moderately hot 200°C (400°F/Gas 6). Grease a 27 cm (11 inch) loose-bottomed flan tin. Roll the dough out between two sheets of baking paper large enough to line the tin. Remove the paper and invert the pastry into the tin. Use a small pastry ball to press the pastry into the tin, allowing any excess to hang over the side. Roll a rolling pin over the tin, cutting off any excess. Cover the pastry with a piece of crumpled baking paper, then add baking beads. Place the tin on a baking tray and bake for 15–20 minutes. Remove the paper and beads, reduce the heat to moderate 180°C (350°F/Gas 4) and bake for 20 minutes, or until golden.

**3** To make the salsa verde, combine all the ingredients in a food processor and process until almost smooth.

**4** Boil the potato until just tender. Drain. Heat the oil in a large frying pan and cook the garlic, capsicum and onion over medium heat for 3 minutes, stirring frequently. Add the zucchini, dill, thyme and capers and cook for 3 minutes. Reduce the heat to low, add the potato and artichokes, and heat through. Season to taste.

**5** To assemble, spread 3 tablespoons of the salsa over the pastry. Spoon the vegetable mixture into the case and drizzle with half the remaining salsa. Pile the spinach in the centre and drizzle with the remaining salsa.

NUTRITION PER SERVE
Protein 7 g; Fat 37 g; Carbohydrate 36 g;
Dietary Fibre 4.5 g; Cholesterol 65 mg;
2110 kJ (505 cal)

Rub the butter into the flour and salt with your fingertips until it resembles fine breadcrumbs.

Mix with a flat-bladed knife until the dough comes together in beads.

Press the pastry gently into the side of the greased flan tin.

Bake the pastry case until it is dry to the touch and golden brown.

Mix together the salsa verde ingredients in a food processor until almost smooth.

Spread salsa verde over the pastry base, then fill with the hot vegetables.

## OLIVE SPIRALS

Preparation time: 25 minutes +
    1 hour 40 minutes rising
Total cooking time: 35 minutes
Makes 12 spirals

7 g (¹/4 oz) dried yeast
1 teaspoon sugar
4 cups (500 g/1 lb) plain flour
1 teaspoon salt
2 tablespoons olive oil
2 cups (250 g/8 oz) pitted black olives
¹/2 cup (50 g/1³/4 oz) finely grated
    Parmesan
3 cloves garlic, chopped
1 tablespoon oil

**1** Mix the yeast, sugar and ¹/2 cup (125 ml/4 fl oz) warm water in a bowl. Cover and set aside in a warm place for 10 minutes, or until frothy.

**2** Sift the flour and salt into a bowl and make a well in the centre. Add the frothy yeast, oil and 1 cup (250 ml/ 8 fl oz) of warm water. Mix to a soft dough and gather into a ball. Turn out onto a floured surface and knead for 10 minutes, or until smooth. Cover loosely with greased plastic wrap and set aside for 1 hour, or until well risen.

**3** Process the olives, Parmesan and garlic in a food processor until chopped. With the motor running, add the tablespoon of oil and process to a paste.

**4** Punch down the dough and knead for 1 minute. Roll out to a rectangle 42 x 35 cm (18 x 14 inches). Spread with the olive paste, leaving a border along one long side. Roll up length-ways, ending with the clear long side.

**5** Cut into 12 slices and place close together on a greased baking tray. Cover with a damp tea towel and set aside for 30 minutes, or until well risen. Preheat the oven to moderately hot 200°C (400°F/Gas 6). Bake for 35 minutes, or until golden brown.

NUTRITION PER SPIRAL
Protein 8 g; Fat 8 g; Carbohydrate 40 g;
Dietary Fibre 3 g; Cholesterol 4 mg;
1050 kJ (250 cal)

Spread the rectangle of dough with olive paste and roll up lengthways.

Using a serrated knife, cut the rolled log into 12 equal slices.

Place the spirals close together on the baking tray so that they touch while cooking.

## BEEF VERMICELLI CAKE

Preparation time: 10 minutes +
  10 minutes standing
Total cooking time: 50 minutes
Serves 4–6

90 g (3 oz) butter
1 onion, chopped
500 g (1 lb) beef mince
800 g (1 lb 10 oz) bottled tomato
  pasta sauce
2 tablespoons tomato paste
250 g (8 oz) vermicelli
1/4 cup (30 g/1 oz) plain flour
1 1/4 cups (315 ml/10 oz) milk
1 1/4 cups (150 g/5 oz) grated
  Cheddar

**1** Preheat the oven to moderate 180°C (350°F/Gas 4). Lightly grease a 24 cm (10 inch) round deep springform tin. Melt a tablespoon of the butter in a large deep frying pan and cook the onion over medium heat for 2–3 minutes, or until soft. Add the beef mince, breaking up any lumps with the back of a spoon, and cook for 4–5 minutes, or until browned. Stir in the pasta sauce and tomato paste, reduce the heat and simmer for 20–25 minutes. Season well.
**2** Cook the pasta in a large pan of rapidly boiling salted water until *al dente*. Drain well and rinse. Meanwhile, melt the remaining butter in a saucepan over low heat. Stir in the flour and cook for 1 minute, or until pale and foaming. Remove from the

heat and gradually stir in the milk. Return to the heat and stir constantly until the sauce boils and thickens. Reduce the heat and simmer for 2 minutes.
**3** Spread half the pasta over the base of the tin, then cover with half the meat sauce. Cover with the remaining pasta, pressing down with the palm of your hand. Spoon on the remaining meat sauce and then pour on the white sauce. Sprinkle with cheese and cook for 15 minutes. Leave to stand for 10 minutes before removing from the tin. Cut into wedges to serve.

NUTRITION PER SERVE (6)
Protein 34 g; Fat 32 g; Carbohydrate 47 g;
Dietary Fibre 6 g; Cholesterol 121 mg;
2535 kJ (605 cal)

Cook the mince until browned, breaking up any lumps with a spoon.

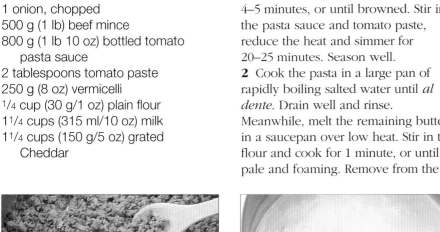
Cook the sauce, stirring, until it comes to the boil and thickens.

Spread half the pasta into the tin and then cover with half the meat sauce.

# PIZZA-TOPPED FOCACCIA

Preparation time: 30 minutes +
   1 hour 30 minutes standing
Total cooking time: 40 minutes
Serves 4

7 g (1/4 oz) sachet dry yeast
1 teaspoon sugar
2 tablespoons olive oil
2 1/2 cups (310 g/10 oz) plain flour,
   sifted

PIZZA TOPPING
1 tablespoon tomato paste
1 large red capsicum, thinly sliced
125 g (4 oz) marinated artichoke
   hearts, quartered
1/4 cup (30 g/1 oz) black olives, pitted
200 g (6 1/2 oz) bocconcini, thickly
   sliced

**1** Combine the yeast, 3/4 cup (185 ml/ 6 fl oz) of warm water and the sugar in a bowl and set aside in a warm place for 5–10 minutes, or until frothy. Put the oil, flour and 1 teaspoon salt in a large bowl, add the frothy yeast and mix to a soft dough.
**2** Turn the dough out onto a lightly floured surface and knead for 10 minutes, or until smooth and elastic. Roll into a ball and place in a large oiled bowl. Cover with oiled plastic wrap and set aside in a warm place for 1 hour, or until the dough has doubled in size.
**3** Preheat the oven to moderate 180°C (350°F/Gas 4). Punch down the dough with your fist to expel any air, and knead for 1 minute. Roll into a flat disc large enough to fit into a greased 23 cm (9 inch) springform tin. Press into the tin, cover with a tea towel and leave to rise for about 20 minutes.

**4** Spread the tomato paste over the dough and arrange the other topping ingredients, except for the bocconcini, on top. Bake for 20 minutes, remove from the oven and spread the slices of bocconcini over the top, then bake for a further 20 minutes, or until the dough is well risen and firm to the touch in the centre. Cool on a wire rack before cutting and serving.

NUTRITION PER SERVE
Protein 25 g; Fat 20 g; Carbohydrate 60 g;
Dietary Fibre 5 g; Cholesterol 30 mg;
2235 kJ (535 Cal)

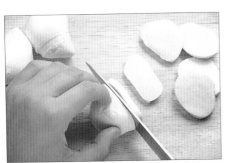

Bocconcini are small balls of mozzarella. Cut them into thick slices with a sharp knife.

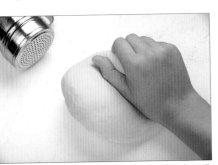

On a lightly floured surface, knead the dough until smooth and elastic.

Arrange the capsicum, artichokes and olives over the tomato paste.

# PESTO AND ANCHOVY TART

Preparation time: 35 minutes
Total cooking time: 30 minutes
Serves 6

**PESTO**
1½ cups (75 g/2½ oz) fresh basil
    leaves, firmly packed
2 cloves garlic
½ cup (50 g/1¾ oz) grated
    Parmesan
½ cup (80 g/2¾ oz) pine nuts,
    toasted
¼ cup (60 ml/2 fl oz) olive oil

375 g (12 oz) block puff pastry
1 egg yolk, lightly beaten
45 g (1½ oz) can anchovies, drained
⅓ cup (50 g/1¾ oz) grated
    mozzarella cheese
⅓ cup (35 g/1¼ oz) grated
    Parmesan

**1** To make the pesto, put the basil, garlic, Parmesan and pine nuts in a food processor and chop finely. With the motor running, add the oil and process until well combined.
**2** Preheat the oven to 200°C (400°F/ Gas 6). Roll the pastry into a rectangle 18 x 35 cm (7 x 14 inches), and 5 mm (¼ inch) thick. Cut a 2 cm (¾ inch) strip from all the way round the edge of the pastry. Combine the lightly beaten egg yolk with 1 teaspoon of water. Use this to brush the edge of the pastry. Trim the pastry strips to fit around the rectangle and attach them to form a crust. Place on a lightly floured baking tray and, using the tip of a sharp knife, make small cuts all over the base. Bake for 15 minutes. Press the centre of the pastry down

with the back of a spoon and bake for a further 5 minutes, or until lightly golden. Allow to cool.
**3** Spread the pesto evenly over the base of the pastry. Cut the anchovies into thin strips and arrange over the pesto. Sprinkle the grated mozzarella

and Parmesan over the top and bake for 10 minutes, or until golden.

NUTRITION PER SERVE
Protein 15 g; Fat 40 g; Carbohydrate 25 g;
Dietary Fibre 2 g; Cholesterol 70 mg;
2155 kJ (515 cal)

Add the olive oil to the chopped basil, garlic, Parmesan and pine nuts.

Attach the strips of pastry around the edge of the rectangle to make a crust.

Spread the pesto evenly into the shaped pastry base.

## MUSHROOM, RICOTTA AND OLIVE PIZZA

Preparation time: 30 minutes + proving
Total cooking time: 1 hour
Serves 6

4 Roma (egg) tomatoes, quartered
3/4 teaspoon caster sugar
7 g (1/4 oz) dry yeast or
    15 g (1/2 oz) fresh yeast
1/2 cup (125 ml/4 fl oz) skim milk
13/4 cups (220 g/7 oz) plain flour
2 teaspoons olive oil
2 cloves garlic, crushed
1 onion, thinly sliced
750 g (11/2 lb) cap mushrooms, sliced
1 cup (250 g/8 oz) ricotta cheese
2 tablespoons sliced black olives
small fresh basil leaves

**1**  Preheat the oven to hot 210°C (415°F/Gas 6–7). Put the tomatoes on a baking tray covered with baking paper, sprinkle with salt, cracked black pepper and 1/2 teaspoon sugar and bake for 20 minutes, or until the edges are starting to darken.
**2**  Stir the yeast and remaining sugar with 3 tablespoons warm water until the yeast dissolves. Cover and leave in a warm place until foamy (if the yeast doesn't foam you will have to throw it away and start again). Warm the milk. Sift the flour into a large bowl and stir in the yeast and milk. Mix to a soft dough, then turn onto a lightly floured surface and knead for 5 minutes. Leave, covered, in a lightly oiled bowl in a warm place for 40 minutes, or until doubled in size.
**3**  Heat the oil in a pan and fry the garlic and onion until soft. Add the mushrooms and stir until they are soft and the liquid has evaporated. Cool.
**4**  Turn the dough out onto a lightly floured surface and knead lightly. Roll out to a 36 cm (15 inch) circle and transfer to a lightly greased oven or pizza tray. Spread with the ricotta, leaving a border to turn over the filling. Top with the mushrooms, leaving a circle in the centre and arrange the tomato and olives in the circle. Fold the dough edge over onto the mushroom and dust the edge with flour. Bake for 25 minutes, or until the crust is golden. Garnish with basil.

NUTRITION PER SERVE
Protein 15 g; Fat 7.5 g; Carbohydrate 30 g;
Dietary Fibre 6 g; Cholesterol 20 mg;
1100 kJ (265 Cal)

Leave the yeast in a warm place until it begins to foam and become active.

Spread the ricotta over the pastry, leaving a border to turn over the filling.

# desserts

# TIRAMISU

Preparation time: 30 minutes +
  2 hours refrigeration
Total cooking time: Nil
Serves 6

3 cups (750 ml/24 fl oz) strong black
  coffee, cooled
3 tablespoons Marsala or
  coffee-flavoured liqueur
2 eggs, separated
3 tablespoons caster sugar
250 g (8 oz) mascarpone
1 cup (250 ml/8 fl oz) cream, whipped
16 large sponge fingers
2 tablespoons dark cocoa powder

**1** Mix together the coffee and Marsala in a bowl and set aside. Using electric beaters, beat the egg yolks and sugar in a bowl for 3 minutes, or until thick and pale. Add the mascarpone and mix until just combined. Transfer to a large bowl and fold in the cream.
**2** Beat the egg whites until soft peaks form. Fold quickly and lightly into the cream mixture.
**3** Dip half the biscuits into the coffee mixture, then drain off any excess coffee and arrange in the base of a 2.5 litre ceramic dish. Spread half the cream mixture over the biscuits.
**4** Dip the remaining biscuits into the remaining coffee mixture and repeat the layers. Smooth the surface and dust liberally with the cocoa powder. Refrigerate for at least 2 hours, or until firm.

NUTRITION PER SERVE
Protein 7.5 g; Fat 24 g; Carbohydrate 28 g; Dietary Fibre 1 g; Cholesterol 180 mg; 1545 kJ (370 cal)

STORAGE: Tiramisu is best made a day in advance to let the flavours develop. Refrigerate until ready to serve.

Fold the beaten egg whites gently into the cream mixture with a metal spoon.

Dip half the biscuits in the coffee mixture, drain, and arrange in the serving dish.

Add the mascarpone to the egg yolks and sugar and mix until just combined.

## STRAWBERRIES WITH BALSAMIC VINEGAR

Preparation time: 10 minutes +
  2 hours 30 minutes marinating
Total cooking time: Nil
Serves 4

750 g (1¹/₂ lb) small ripe strawberries
¹/₄ cup (60 g/2 oz) caster sugar
2 tablespoons balsamic vinegar
¹/₂ cup (125 g/4 oz) mascarpone

**1** Wipe the strawberries with a clean damp cloth and carefully remove the green stalks. If the strawberries are large, cut each one in half.
**2** Place all the strawberries in a large glass bowl, sprinkle the caster sugar evenly over the top and toss gently to coat. Set aside for 2 hours to macerate, then sprinkle the balsamic vinegar over the strawberries. Toss them again, then refrigerate for about 30 minutes.
**3** Spoon the strawberries into four glasses, drizzle with the syrup and top with a dollop of mascarpone.

NUTRITION PER SERVE
Protein 6 g; Fat 11 g; Carbohydrate 20 g; Dietary Fibre 4 g; Cholesterol 30 mg; 830 kJ (200 cal)

NOTE: If you leave the strawberries for more than 2 hours, it is best to refrigerate them.

Hull the strawberries after wiping clean with a damp cloth.

Sprinkle the caster sugar evenly over the strawberries and toss to coat.

Use good-quality balsamic vinegar to sprinkle over the strawberries.

## LEMON GRANITA

Preparation time: 15 minutes + 2 hours
   freezing
Total cooking time: 5 minutes
Serves 6

1¼ cups (315 ml/10 fl oz) lemon juice
1 tablespoon lemon zest
200 g (6½ oz) caster sugar

**1** Place the lemon juice, lemon zest and caster sugar in a small saucepan and stir over low heat for 5 minutes, or until the sugar is dissolved. Remove from the heat and leave to cool.
**2** Add 2 cups (500 ml/16 fl oz) water to the juice mixture and mix together well. Pour the mixture into a shallow 30 x 20 cm (12 x 8 inch) metal container and place in the freezer until the mixture is beginning to freeze around the edges. Scrape the frozen sections back into the mixture with a fork. Repeat every 30 minutes until the mixture has even-size ice crystals. Beat the mixture with a fork just before serving. To serve, spoon the lemon granita into six chilled glasses.

NUTRITION PER SERVE
Protein 0 g; Fat 0 g; Carbohydrate 35 g;
Dietary Fibre 0 g; Cholesterol 0 mg;
592 kJ (140 cal)

Stir the juice, zest and sugar over low heat until the sugar has dissolved.

Scrape the frozen edges of the mixture back into the centre.

Beat the granita mixture with a fork just prior to serving to break up the crystals.

# BERRY RICOTTA CREAM TARTLETS

Preparation time: 1 hour + 1 hour refrigeration
Total cooking time: 40 minutes
Serves 6

1¹/₂ cups (185 g/6 oz) plain flour
¹/₂ cup (90 g/3 oz) ground almonds
¹/₃ cup (40 g/1¹/₄ oz) icing sugar
125 g (4 oz) unsalted butter, chilled and cubed
1 egg, lightly beaten

FILLING
200 g (6¹/₂ oz) ricotta
1 teaspoon vanilla essence
2 eggs
²/₃ cup (160 g/5¹/₂ oz) caster sugar
¹/₂ cup (125 ml/4 fl oz) cream
¹/₂ cup (60 g/2 oz) raspberries
¹/₂ cup (80 g/2³/₄ oz) blueberries
icing sugar, to dust

**1** Sift the flour into a large bowl, then add the almonds and icing sugar. Rub the butter into the flour with your fingertips until it resembles fine breadcrumbs. Make a well in the centre and add the egg and mix with a flat-bladed knife, using a cutting action, until the mixture comes together in beads. Turn out onto a lightly floured work surface and gather into a ball. Wrap in plastic and refrigerate for 30 minutes.
**2** Grease six 8 cm (3 inch) loose-based tart tins. Roll out the pastry between two sheets of baking paper to fit the base and side of the tins, trimming away the excess. Prick the bases with a fork, then refrigerate for 30 minutes. Preheat the oven to 180°C (350°F/Gas 4).

**3** Line the pastry bases with baking paper and spread with a layer of baking beads or rice. Bake for 8–10 minutes and then remove the paper and beads.
**4** Mix the ricotta, vanilla essence, eggs, sugar and cream in a food processor until smooth.
**5** Divide the berries and filling among

the tarts and bake for 25–30 minutes, or until the filling is just set—the top should be soft but not too wobbly. Cool. Dust with icing sugar to serve.

NUTRITION PER SERVE
Protein 14 g; Fat 42 g; Carbohydrate 62 g; Dietary Fibre 3.5 g; Cholesterol 187 mg; 2780 kJ (665 cal)

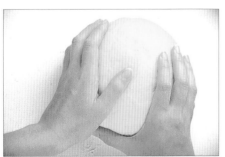
Gently gather the dough together and press into a ball. Wrap in plastic and refrigerate.

Roll out the pastry between two sheets of baking paper to prevent sticking.

Divide the berries among the pastry cases and then pour in the filling over the top.

# HONEY AND PINE NUT TART

Preparation time: 25 minutes +
  15 minutes refrigeration
Total cooking time: 1 hour
Serves 6

2 cups (250 g/8 oz) plain flour
1¹/₂ tablespoons icing sugar
115 g (4 oz) unsalted butter, chilled
  and cubed
1 egg, lightly beaten
2 tablespoons iced water

FILLING
1¹/₂ cups (235 g/7¹/₂ oz) pine nuts
¹/₂ cup (180 g/6 oz) honey
115 g (4 oz) unsalted butter, softened
¹/₂ cup (125 g/4 oz) caster sugar
3 eggs, lightly beaten
¹/₄ teaspoon vanilla essence
1 tablespoon almond liqueur
1 teaspoon finely grated lemon rind
1 tablespoon lemon juice
icing sugar, for dusting

**1**  Preheat the oven to 190°C (375°F/ Gas 5) and place a baking tray on the middle shelf. Lightly grease a 23 x 3.5 cm (9 x 1¹/₂ inch) deep loose-based tart tin. Sift the flour and icing sugar into a large bowl and add the butter. Rub in the butter with your fingertips until the mixture resembles fine breadcrumbs. Make a well in the centre and add the egg and water. Mix with a flat-bladed knife, using a cutting action, until the dough comes together in beads.

**2**  Turn out onto a lightly floured work surface and press together into a ball. Roll out to a circle 3 mm (¹/₈ inch) thick to line the tin and trim away any excess pastry. Prick the base all over with a fork and chill for 15 minutes. Cut out leaves from the trimmings for decoration. Cover and chill.

**3**  Line the pastry with baking paper and spread with a layer of baking beads or rice. Bake on the heated tray for 10 minutes, then remove.

**4**  Reduce the oven to 180°C (350°F/ Gas 4). To make the filling, spread the pine nuts on a baking tray and roast in the oven for 3 minutes, or until golden. Heat the honey in a small

saucepan until runny. Beat the butter and sugar in a bowl until smooth and pale. Gradually add the eggs, beating well after each addition. Mix in the honey, vanilla, liqueur, lemon rind and juice and a pinch of salt. Stir in the pine nuts, spoon into the pastry case and smooth the surface. Arrange the pastry leaves in the centre.

**5**  Place on the hot tray and bake for 40 minutes, or until golden and set. Cover the top with foil after

25 minutes. Serve warm, dusted with icing sugar, perhaps with crème fraîche or mascarpone cheese.

NUTRITION PER SERVE
Protein 14 g; Fat 63 g; Carbohydrate 83 g;
Dietary Fibre 3.5 g; Cholesterol 217 mg;
3936 kJ (940 cal)

NOTE: The filling rises and cracks during baking but settles down as the tart cools.

Use a small ball of pastry to press the pastry into the base and side of the tin.

Arrange the pastry leaves over the smoothed pine nut filling.

# FLOURLESS CHOCOLATE CAKE

Preparation time: 1 hour + overnight
    refrigeration
Total cooking time: 1 hour 15 minutes
Serves 10

500 g (1 lb) good-quality dark
    chocolate, chopped
6 eggs
2 tablespoons Frangelico or brandy
1½ cups (165 g/5½ oz) ground
    hazelnuts
1 cup (250 ml/8 fl oz) cream, whipped
icing sugar, to dust
thick cream, to serve (optional)

**1** Preheat the oven to slow 150°C (300°F/Gas 2). Grease a deep 20 cm (8 inch) round cake tin and line the base with baking paper.
**2** Half-fill a saucepan with water and bring to the boil. Remove from the heat and sit the chocolate in a heatproof bowl over the pan, making sure it is not touching the water. Stir occasionally until melted.
**3** Put the eggs in a large heatproof bowl and add the Frangelico. Place the bowl over a saucepan of just simmering water on low heat, making sure the bowl does not touch the water. Beat the mixture with electric beaters on high speed for 7 minutes, or until light and foamy. Remove from the heat.
**4** Using a metal spoon, quickly and lightly fold the chocolate and nuts into the egg mixture until just combined. Fold in the cream and pour into the cake tin. Place the tin in a shallow roasting tin. Pour enough hot water into the roasting tin to come halfway up the side of the cake tin. Bake for 1 hour, or until just set. Remove from the roasting tin and cool to room temperature. Cover with plastic wrap and refrigerate overnight.
**5** Invert the cake onto a plate and remove the baking paper. Cut into slices, dust lightly with icing sugar and serve with thick cream.

NUTRITION PER SERVE
Protein 9 g; Fat 38 g; Carbohydrate 34 g;
Dietary Fibre 2.5 g; Cholesterol 142 mg;
2135 kJ (510 Cal)

Grease the cake tin with butter or brush with oil, and line the base with baking paper.

Beat the mixture over simmering water until light and foamy.

Gently fold the whipped cream into the chocolate nut mixture.

Place the cake tin in the roasting tin and bake until just set.

# Glossary

**Anchovies** are a small fish from the herring family found mainly in southern European waters. Although they can be eaten fresh, they are rarely found outside Mediterranean fishing ports. More commonly, they are cured and packed in oil, salt or brine and are readily availalbe in cans or jars.

**Arborio rice** is a special plump, short-grained rice used for making risotto.

**Balsamic vinegar** is a rich, sweet and fragrant vinegar originating from Modena in Italy. Often used in dressings.

**Bicarbonate of soda** (baking soda)

**Buttermilk** is a low-fat milk with a characteristic tang.

**Bocconcini** are small balls of fresh Italian mozzarella available from delicatessens. Keep refrigerated and covered in the whey in which they are sold for up to 3 weeks. Discard if they show signs of yellowing.

**Borlotti beans** are slightly kidney-shaped, large, pale pink beans beautifully marked with burgundy specks. They are sometimes available fresh, otherwise canned or dried can be used.

**Broad beans** (fava beans)

**Calamari** (squid)

**Cannellini beans** (white beans, Italian white beans) are white, kidney-shaped beans. They are available fresh, canned or dried.

**Capers** are the pickled buds of a shrub that grows wild in many parts of the Mediterranean. Capers have a sharp, sour taste and are sold in seasoned vinegar or packed in salt which needs to be rinsed off before use.

**Capsicum** (pepper)

**Caster sugar** (superfine sugar) is a fine white sugar with very small crystals.

**Clams** (vongole)

**Conchigliette** are a small shell-shaped pasta often used in soups.

**Cornflour** (cornstarch)

**Cos** (romaine lettuce)

**Eggplants** (aubergines) come in a variety of shapes, sizes and colours. Slender eggplants are also called baby, finger or Japanese eggplants, while the most commonly used are larger and rounder.

**English spinach** (spinach) is sometimes confused with Swiss chard but is much more tender and delicate. Requires little to no cooking but should be washed several times to remove dirt.

**Feta cheese** is a soft, fresh white cheese ripened in brine. Originally made from the milk of sheep or goats, but often now made with the more economical cow's milk. Feta cheese tastes salty and sharp.

**Flat-leaf parsley** (Italian parsley, Continental parsley)

**French shallots** are members of the onion family but have a sweeter flavour.

**Gorgonzola cheese** is a blue cheese.

**Green beans** (French beans, string beans)

**Icing sugar** (confectioners' sugar, powdered sugar). Made by grinding granulated sugar to a fine powder.

**Mascarpone cheese** is a soft fresh cheese made with cream to which citric or tartaric acid has been added.

**Mince** (ground meat)

**Olive oil** comes in different varieties suitable for different purposes. Extra virgin or virgin olive oil are most commonly used in dressings. Regular olive oils are preferred for cooking because of their neutral flavour. Light olive oil refers to the low content of extra virgin olive oil rather than lightness of calories.

**Parmesan** is a hard cow's milk cheese used widely in Italian cooking. Sold either grated or in blocks, freshly grated has a much better flavour. Parmigiano Reggiano, from Parma in Northern Italy, is the most superior Parmesan.

**Pecorino cheese** is one of Italy's most popular cheeses, with virtually every region producing its own variety. Pecorino is made from sheep's milk.

**Plain flour** (all-purpose flour)

**Polenta** (cornmeal) is ground dried corn kernels and is a staple in Northern Italy. Polenta is often made into a porridge and flavoured by mixing in butter and Parmesan cheese.

**Prawns** (shrimp) are crustaceans which come in various sizes and colours. They become opaque and turn pink once cooked.

**Prosciutto** is an Italian ham that has been cured by salting then drying in the air. Aged for up to ten months, it is then sliced thinly. It does not require cooking. Prosiutto di Parma is the classic Italian ham traditionally served as an antipasto and also used extensively in cooking.

**Risoni** is a small rice-shaped pasta often used in soups.

**Rocket** (arugula, rugula, roquette) is a leaf with a peppery flavour that becomes more pronounced the older the leaf. Often used in salads.

**Roma tomatoes** (egg tomatoes, plum tomatoes) are favoured for canning and drying because they have few seeds and a dry flesh. Ideal in sauces and purées. Sometimes called Italian tomatoes.

**Semi-dried tomatoes** (sun-blushed tomatoes) are widely available in oil.

**Spring onion** (scallion, shallot). These immature onions have a mild, delicate flavour, and both the green tops and the white bulbs can be eaten raw or cooked.

**Thick cream** (double cream, heavy cream) has a minimum fat content of 48% and some brands have gelatine added to them to give more body.

**Tomato paste** (tomato purée, double concentrate)

**Vanilla essence** (vanilla extract) is made by steeping vanilla beans in alcohol and water. Look for products marked natural vanilla or pure vanilla extract and avoid the cheaper synthetic vanilla flavouring which is made from the chemical artificial vanillan.

**Zucchini** (courgette)

# Index

Published by Murdoch Books®, a division of Murdoch Magazines Pty Ltd.

Murdoch Books® Australia
GPO Box 1203
Sydney NSW 2001
Phone: + 61 (0) 2 4352 7000
Fax: + 61 (0) 2 4352 7026

Murdoch Books UK Limited
Ferry House
51-57 Lacy Road
Putney, London SW15 1PR
Phone: + 44 (0) 20 8355 1480
Fax: + 44 (0) 20 8355 1499

Editorial Director: Diana Hill
Project Manager: Zoë Harpham
Creative Director: Marylouise Brammer
Designer: Michelle Cutler
Production: Fiona Byrne
Recipes developed by the Murdoch Books Test Kitchen.

Chief Executive: Juliet Rogers
Publisher: Kay Scarlett

The Publisher gratefully acknowledges the contribution of the recipe writers, chefs,
photographers and stylists who worked on the material appearing in this publication.

National Library of Australia Cataloguing-in-Publication Data
Everyday Italian. Includes index. ISBN 1 74045 207 0.
1. Cookery, Italian. (Series: Everyday series (Sydney, NSW)).
641.5945

IMPORTANT: Those who might be at risk from the effects of salmonella food poisoning
(the elderly, pregnant women, young children and those suffering from immune deficiency diseases)
should consult their GP with any concerns about eating raw eggs.